Advance Praise for

FIVE FOR YOUR FIRST FIVE

Dr. Allison McWilliams has hit the nail right on the head and provides focused, effective and actionable ideas for recent college grads who are getting too much inspiration and too little useable help addressing the substantial challenge of building their lives after college. Much of the literature for this audience patronizingly over-compliments them ("You are amazing and can do anything!") or over-criticizes them ("Today's young adults are so entitled - they're impossible!"). Neither of these categorizations is accurate or helpful - quite the opposite. Dr. McWilliams distills her substantial experience in working in some of the most advanced career-preparatory institutions in the country well by picking five key areas for grads to focus their efforts in building a life they own and can love. Her assessments of what's needed directly complements our decade-plus of work in the Stanford Life Design Lab. Her counsel spans the wide swath of necessary critical skills ranging from forming deep habits of personal reflection to navigating the tactical constraints of that tough first job out of college many grads will get. She tells it like it is without making assumptions or judgments about her reader and balances artfully conversing with her reader and challenging them via exercises to do the work. Like Dr. McWilliams, our team believes that successfully journeying those first five years after graduation (and defining what success is wisely!) is terrifically important. If you love anyone who is currently or about to be in those five years, do them the kindness of giving them this book.

Dave Evans
Co-Author, New York Times #1 Bestseller *Designing Your Life*,
and
Co-Founder, *Stanford Life Design Lab*

D1463143

Five For Your First Five

FIVE FOR YOUR FIRST FIVE

Own Your Career and Life After College

by

Allison E. McWilliams

library partners press

a digital publishing imprint

First Edition, First Printing

ISBN 978-1618460431

Copyright © 2017 by Allison E. McWilliams

Cover designed by Lauren R. Beam

Produced and Distributed By:

Library Partners Press
ZSR Library
Wake Forest University
1834 Wake Forest Road
Winston-Salem, North Carolina 27106

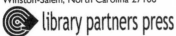 library partners press

a digital publishing imprint

www.librarypartnerspress.org

Manufactured in the United States of America

ABOUT THIS BOOK

Young adults making their way from college to life-after-college face a multitude of decisions, challenges, and opportunities. How do you build skills and experiences that will benefit you in the future, when you are on the lowest rung of the professional ladder? How do you balance creating a life with professional demands when your time is not your own? How do you ensure you are practicing self-care – physically, mentally, financially, and emotionally – when you don't know what the resources are to do that? How do you build your network and find mentors? And, how do you take ownership for what comes next?

These and many others are the questions that all young professionals should be asking themselves, especially in the critical first five years out of college. This is the time when you will discover more about yourself than at any other point in your life. You will discover strengths, interests, and beliefs that will guide your future career and life decisions. You will learn professional and life skills and habits that will be the foundation for your future professional selves. You will begin to discern what matters to you, and begin to define what a meaningful life looks like, for you. And, you largely will be expected to do all of this work on your own.

FIVE FOR YOUR FIRST FIVE is based on twenty years of experience working with college students and young adults as they make this sometimes challenging and overwhelming transition from college to life-after-college. It combines real-life stories and experiences, from young adults who have already navigated through these waters, with tools, strategies, discussion, and reflection questions. The reader is encouraged to do real, intentional work while exploring the five key areas: Do the Work, Build a Life, Create Community, Practice Reflection, and Own What's Next. Part workbook, part wise counselor and mentor, FIVE FOR YOUR FIRST FIVE provides meaningful insight into what can happen when you truly take ownership for your career and life.

FOREWORD

Nathan O. Hatch
President, Wake Forest University

IN THE SUMMER OF 2017, David Brooks wrote, "Mis-Educating the Young," a column in the *New York Times* that questioned how we educate young people and if we actually prepare them for life. Acknowledging the tumultuous years following college, Brooks posed the question: "How do we, as a society, prepare young people for this uncertain phase?" In this book, Dr. Allison McWilliams offers valuable suggestions in response to that question.

Since arriving at Wake Forest in 2010, Allison has taken a relational, face-to-face campus culture and applied it to personal and career development. She has been part of a creative team in the Office of Personal and Career Development, which Wake Forest had established as a major University priority. Under the direction of Vice President Andy Chan, this office has taken bold steps to help students navigate the transition from college to the world of work.

Allison's important work in mentoring has grown beyond our campus and extends across the country to our alumni. Hundreds have participated in personal and development programs, including young professional mentoring groups, an intensive, nine-month process dedicated to reflecting on personal and professional challenges, successes and opportunities. For the last five years, conversations with these groups revealed similar concerns and questions, common challenges and uncertainties among young professionals, and ultimately, inspired Allison to put her insights on paper.

As the theory learned in college classrooms turns to practice in real life, young professionals are caught in a time of transition. It is a season for them to navigate and explore, test themselves and challenge their own fortitude, and Allison offers an honest, candid and compassionate voice on the journey. She invites the reader into a conversation that leaves you feeling understood and armed with practical suggestions and concrete next steps.

The world is asking young people to take what they've learned in school and apply it to their lives. Critical thinking, problem solving and clear communication were not just meant for science experiments or historical analysis. These skills are foundational to life outside of school and the many years to follow.

The time after college should not simply be focused on securing a job; it should be dedicated to building a life. This is an opportunity to intentionally and holistically devote time and thought to who you are, who you want to be, what you do and what you want to be doing. It is a chance to create and discover meaning and purpose in your life.

The refreshing part for young professionals reading this book is that you are not alone. You and your friends are probably experiencing some of the same things. Ask them about it; share your thoughts with them. There are also others you can reach out to who have made it through this time – your parents, a mentor, other friends and family. What lessons do they have from their experience that might help you? You don't have to have all of the answers; you just have to be willing to keep learning, asking questions and exploring.

I recall my own vocational quest in the first years after college. It was intense and demanding as I wrestled with what direction to take and which graduate school to pursue. I ended up pursuing a doctorate in American history. In that process, friends and family were crucial in keeping things in perspective, in reminding me of my own gifts and talents, and in supporting the decisions that were made.

As you take time to read this book and reflect on your circumstances, enjoy the process of intentionally thinking about your life. And above all, take time to enjoy the life you're living. I wish you the best.

Nathan O. Hatch
President, Wake Forest University
Fall 2017

CONTENTS

INTRODUCTION

Is This All There Is?

A few years ago, I was talking with a young woman named Liz, who was participating in a young-professional mentoring group I was facilitating. By all appearances, Liz was happy and enjoying some early post college successes. She had a great job and was well liked by her colleagues and her superiors. She was living in a big urban area, where she had chosen to move, which offered lots of opportunities to meet new people outside of work as well as to connect with friends from college. She was making good money and was able to support herself. But all of these seemingly positive aspects to her life masked an ongoing internal struggle that, after several months, Liz finally was able to articulate: "I like my job. I'm learning things, I like being challenged, and I like my coworkers. But I find myself wondering, is this all there is?"

This bit of existential crisis, this questioning, "Is this all there is?" is representative of the young adults whom I see and talk to on a regular basis. To some it may sound like whining or an unwillingness to "pay their dues." Indeed, over the past few years a lot has been written about this generation of young people, as they enter and make their ways through their first professional roles. They're flighty. They have no work ethic. They lack commitment. They're disconnected (from people). They're too connected (to technology). They're self-centered. And so on.

While these descriptors (and many more, I'm sure) may be representative of any number of individuals, I do not see the young people whom I work with and encounter on a regular basis reflected in this list. Instead, what I see are young people who have been told their entire lives, "You can do anything you want," but have not been given the direction, guidance, or tools to figure out how to get there, or the feedback on why that's not necessarily true.

I see young people who have been taught that their voice matters, and that they should use it, but not given the hard truth about when one should speak up and when one should shut up, and the power and wisdom that comes from knowing the difference. I see young people who are *deeply* reflective about their lives, who ask, "Is this all there is?" not because they are ungrateful for the opportunities they have before them, but because they want to live their lives in intentional ways, and being told "you can do anything you want" has led to a deep paralysis of indecision.

The young people I meet and talk to are begging for someone to advise them on their choices. A lifetime of tutors and other support systems to ensure they can't possibly fail, pressure to overachieve, and being taught to the test has resulted in a deep fear of making the wrong decision, now that they have the freedom and the opportunity to make decisions for themselves. They lack the understanding of how to achieve "success" when they find there are no grading rubrics for life.

When I graduated from college, a million years ago in the mid-1990s, I don't remember struggling with these same issues. We went to college, we then went to graduate school or got a job, and we were grateful for whatever we got. And it's not because we were better people than those who are graduating now, but we were certainly less reflective ones.

We didn't question what might happen after college, or whether our goals aligned with our strengths and interests, because no one was telling us we should be doing those things. No one was telling us, "You can do anything you want," and we certainly never received a trophy for just showing up to life. So, no, we weren't better people, but there's a part of me that wonders if we weren't better off. We didn't feel the pressure I see in today's students and young adults because we didn't know we should.

What I have learned over the past twenty years of working in higher education, with faculty, staff, students, and alumni, is that the question my young friend Liz asked, "Is this all there is?" is perhaps the *most* important question we *all* can and should be asking ourselves. And it's never too early, nor too late, to start asking that question. **We each get this one life**, and it's up to each of us to spend it in the ways that bring us meaning, in whatever ways we each individually define it.

Which brings me to you, and your individual career and life journey. Sure, there will be loads of people along the way who will have opinions on what you should be doing and how and with whom. Mostly this will be well-intentioned advice, though not all of it will be. Ask a hundred different people for advice on what you should be doing with your life, and you will get a hundred different opinions.

Ultimately, the choice is yours. Now is the time for you to **own your career and your life**. There is literally no other person on this planet who is going to care about your life, and your choices, as much as you. There are many whom you will encounter over the next few years who have better perspective than you do about what will best help you to create a fulfilling life in the long term, and you will need to be intentional about creating relationships with them and learning from them. Your life is something you can let happen *to you*, or it's something you can own. The choice is yours. The choice is always yours.

Over these past years working with young professionals I have had countless conversations, both one-on-one and in group settings, about what owning your work and your life means. These conversations have centered on many of the following questions:

- How do you build skills and experiences that will benefit you in the future, when you are on the lowest rung of the professional ladder, or in a job that doesn't seem to be going anywhere?
- How do you start to identify your values, strengths, and interests and discern how your professional and personal choices are (or are not) aligning with those?
- How do you balance creating a life with professional demands when your time is not your own?
- How do you make sure you are practicing self-care—physically, mentally, financially, and emotionally—when you don't know what the resources are to do that or you don't feel you have the time?
- How do you build community and find friends?
- How do you build your network and find mentors?
- How (and why) do you practice reflection and lifelong learning when you're no longer in school and being forced to do so through your classes?
- How do you take ownership for what comes next?

These are the questions I believe all young professionals should be asking themselves, especially in these critical first five years out of college. Why are they so critical?[1] In these first few years, you arguably will discover more about yourself than you will at any other point in your life. You will discover strengths, interests, and beliefs that will guide your future decisions. You will learn professional and life skills and habits that will be the foundation for your future professional self. You will begin to discern what matters to you, and begin to define what a meaningful life looks like, for you.

This book is a way of exploring these topics and questions and giving you a guide by which you can start to answer them for yourself. In these pages are the **five key areas** that I believe are the most essential to these first five years after graduation, the *Five For Your First Five*. And, significant as these first five years are, I would argue that these are the five key areas we *all* should be working on, whatever our stages of life. I know these are the areas I am constantly thinking about and working on in my own life, even twenty years into my career, as I figure out what matters to me, what's next, and is this—this work, this life—truly all there is.

How to Read This Book

This book has been written as a workbook and is meant to be read interactively. Although it is intended to be read in order, with each chapter building upon the one that preceded it, you, as the reader, should feel free to move about as needed. After all, this is your life we're talking about here. You know what you need, when you need it.

Each chapter provides a combination of tools, strategies, stories from real life experiences, discussion, and reflection questions. While nothing can take the place of an in-person mentoring relationship (more on that later), the goal here is to give you, the reader, the experience of being here, with me, as we explore these issues and questions of life and work.

Have a pen with you as you read, and make note of the things that jump out at you and give you pause. At the end you will find a few blank pages for **Key Takeaways, Ideas, and Action Items**. This is a space for you to jot down notes, interesting concepts, ideas that challenge you, and action items you would like to pursue. Throughout you will find activities for you to work through. **Take the time to do this work.** At the end of each chapter are reflection questions to encourage you to reflect further on the themes and messages of the chapter.

If you have a mentor, ask if he or she would be willing to read it alongside you; as you do, discuss the key learning moments you are having. (If you don't have a mentor, in chapter 3 you will learn more about how to find one.) As John Maxwell has noted, "the greatest achievers in life are people who set goals for themselves and then work hard to reach them. What they *get* by reaching the goals is not nearly as important as what they *become* by reaching them."[2] Intentional reflection, on its own, is a great practice to incorporate into your own development. Intentional reflection in concert with another person will lead to massive growth and learning.

To frame our conversation, I would like for you to remember some key phrases, which are your five for your first five:

1. Do the Work.
2. Build a Life.
3. Create Community.
4. Practice Reflection.
5. Own What's Next.

Do the Work. The book starts with the idea of gaining real work experience. The first few years out of college can feel particularly jarring as the day-to-day realities of entry-level jobs collide with preconceived expectations of what that experience might look or feel like. How do you take ownership for your experience and make sure you are getting out of it what you should be? How do you start to build your post college résumé? How do you claim your voice and your space within your organization?

Your first job is rarely ever going to be the dream job (How depressing that would be! You have nothing else to work for!), but it is a critical time to start discovering strengths, interests, and skills for the future. This is also the time to start examining what you do and don't like about work and how these relate to where you want to be in the future. First and foremost, everything during this time starts and ends with the work you will do. It's imperative you show up every day, ready to give your all, to learn, to grow, and to make the best impression on your coworkers and superiors you possibly can make.

Build a Life. The second chapter is about creating positive life habits. Some of these are practical issues around finances, retirement planning, and finding doctors and other support systems. But others are a bit less obvious. These include questions like how you will spend your time, when it is completely your own? How do you find and create hobbies? What are those individual personal habits you value, and how will you prioritize those in an already-full day? What happens when things don't go exactly as you had planned them, and there is no safety net?

The great gift of being an adult is *you* get to decide how you spend your time and whom you spend it with. The great burden of being an adult is *you do have to decide*. This chapter explores these issues and provides some practical strategies for working through it all and beginning to create the life *you* want to create.

Create Community. Related to this point, the next chapter is all about building community. We all need to feel like we belong to a place. However long you *intend* to live somewhere, you need to *live where you live*. That means putting down roots, joining groups, and building intentional relationships. It means adopting an attitude of permanence. This chapter looks at how you do that, and why it matters.

Just like in the previous chapter where we discuss your ability to choose *how* you spend your time, as an adult you also get to choose *with whom* you spend that time. And it's so critical—both personally *and* professionally— that you make the choices that are right for you, choosing people who align with your values and interests. Creating community means finding adult friends, being intentional about whom you are letting into your life and why, and building a robust, diverse network of mentors and advisers who can help you to explore the decisions and choices you are making.

Practice Reflection. In chapter 4 we explore the power of reflection and lifelong learning. Really, this entire book is about encouraging you to be reflective: reflecting on the choices and decisions you are making, why you are making them, and what you are learning about yourself along the way. This is such a valuable part of your growth and development as an adult, and so intentional reflective strategies have been built into each of the five chapters to encourage you to begin this practice.

Mentoring relationships, in particular, are all about reflective practices, taking intentional stock of where you are, where you have been, and where you are headed. This is work you can do on your own, of course, but it is far too easy to brush it aside for "more important" work that fills up the to-do list and inbox. But if you're not learning from where you have been, you are destined to repeat the mistakes of your past. In this chapter you will look at how you can practice mindfulness in your personal and professional lives, be open to feedback, and identify your strengths and opportunities for growth.

Own What's Next. Finally, the book will conclude with a discussion of how to take each of these intentional practices into your future. Your career and your life don't stop at year five. At some point during the next few years you will likely be forced to choose between safety, comfort, and known success, and uncertainty, risk, and potential failure. This may be a choice you seek out, based on what you would have learned about yourself, your values, your strengths, and your skills. Or, you may have an opportunity that appears unexpectedly, maybe even before you think you are ready for it. Either way, you can start to do some planning now, to put yourself in the best possible position to assess these choices when they appear. In this chapter you will do some intentional preparation for what comes next, in your career and in your life.

Not all of the advice contained in these pages will be applicable to all individuals in all situations, of course, nor will all of your needs and concerns be covered here. If anything, I hope that by reading this book it will encourage you to take ownership of your future, which means you will need to **take individual responsibility to seek out the resources and the information you need.** No one book, resource, or mentor is going to provide you with all of the answers you are seeking, nor should it. That's not what owning your life is about.

For some of you, you are just working a job to pay off student loans, and are not quite ready to think about values and meaning and owning your future. You may not see yourself in the stories shared here. That's fine! I think it is necessary work to recognize the place of privilege that allows some of us to contemplate these things. It's important to recognize that we don't all feel like we are intentionally choosing the lives we are living. *And*, I hope if you are reading this, it will encourage you to think a little bit deeper about what you are experiencing and why. Even if you're just "working a job," you can still derive meaning from it, intentionally develop skills and abilities, and set goals for what comes next.

You may find things in here you disagree with, that are surprising to you, or challenge how you were thinking about your work and your life. That's great! You are the expert on your life and your experience. Don't dismiss those moments, but use them as an opportunity to reflect, to ask why, and to think about what you do with that information as you move forward. Find someone, or a group of someone's, with whom you can discuss those learning moments. That is the value of mentorship and how you learn and grow.

College is fun. College is spending time with great friends, going to parties, going to football games, finding new interests, studying abroad, and sure, going to class. Your number-one job in college was to be a college student. The sociologist Jeffrey Arnett[3] has coined the phrase "emerging adulthood" to describe this period between adolescence and adulthood that generally coincides with the college years. This is a really significant developmental phase, "a time in life when many different directions remain possible, when little about the future has been decided for certain, when the scope of independent exploration of life's possibilities is greater for most people than it will be at any other period of the life course." You may have felt this yourself; this sense of unlimited possibilities and options.

And then there is that moment, at the end, after graduation, after all of the pomp and circumstance, after you pack up your things and say your good-byes for the last time, when you have to go out into the world and create a life for yourself. And there is very little in your previous existence that has prepared you for that moment. Stepping into the adult world after college is exciting, unsettling, challenging, terrifying, exhilarating, exhausting, and about a hundred other adjectives you might be feeling right about now.

As a young professional said to me recently, "Where is the playbook on this stuff?" Well, I hope you will take this book as a guide, as a supportive friend, as a colleague, and a mentor, to help you to navigate your path with a little more certainty, a little more confidence, and a little more clarity about where you might go and how you will get there. **You get this one life**, and only you get to live it. This is the fun part. This is your life! Let's get started.

CHAPTER 1: DO THE WORK

This Is Not the Dream Job

Meet Alexa. She's twenty-four, from Atlanta, and two years into her first professional role post college as a sales assistant for a national magazine in New York. It was a "stepping-stone" job, something to get her to New York and into the magazine business, which is where she thought she wanted to be. Her hope was to move into the marketing side of things fairly quickly, since she didn't have a lot of interest in sales. Prior to graduation she did one summer internship at her dad's company in their marketing department, and a summer internship in the PR department of a hospital. But she figured getting some sales experience would be good for her, and be a great foot in the door. Plus she wanted to be in New York, she thought. But now that she's there, she finds the sales job, not to mention the magazine industry, is not as glamorous or as fun as she thought it would be. She's asked for more responsibility but so far it hasn't been encouraged or supported by the higher-ups. She's barely covering her bills and her parents still have to help her out with her rent in the two-bedroom apartment she is sharing with two friends. She's wondering where this is all going (as do her parents). When she imagined her life after college, in the big city, she didn't imagine she would be working this hard, or struggling this much. And, she can't see a way forward or what she might do next.

S ound familiar? It's a story I hear again and again from young professionals in their first positions out of college. The work isn't as fulfilling as they imagined it would be. The rewards are few, if any. No one ever gives them any sort of positive feedback or any feedback at all. A lot of the time they feel like they have no idea what they're doing, and the rest of the time they aren't being challenged. And, there seems to be no end in sight. Day after day, it's the same thing, for eight or ten or twelve (or more) hours a day.

A big part of this issue stems from a combination of the world you and your peers have just left and the one you have just entered. For the entirety of your life, you have been told the following:

- You are the most important person here.
- Your voice matters, and we want to hear it.
- You are a winner, even when you're not.
- You have all of the resources, support, and guidance you can ever need—we will not let you fail.
- You can be anything you want to be.

Not only have these messages resulted in a good bit of inflated ego, and some unrealistic expectations, which can clash with those of colleagues and supervisors, but they have done you a huge disservice in that they do not remotely prepare you for the world beyond college. There, you are more likely to hear the following:

- You are the *least* important person here.
- You don't know enough yet to have a voice.
- You will be a winner when you prove you are one.
- You need to find your own resources and support—no one here is going to hand it to you.
- You're lucky to have a job.

Of course, this isn't *every* young professional's experience, and it certainly may not be yours. Many young adults are thriving and fully enjoying their lives and first professional positions post college. Many are discovering new talents or interests and enjoying the freedom of living on one's own and learning to make adult decisions about spending and saving, building a career, and developing adult relationships.

But it happens often enough, this disconnect between pre-graduation expectations and post-graduation reality and the resulting frustration, that it seems worthy of focus here. And, no matter how happy you are, or how successful you feel, everyone can benefit from thinking about how to take ownership of these first few years out of college to maximize personal and professional benefit. This is the time for you to think about the following:

- **Who are you and what matters to you?**
- **How are you taking ownership for your career development?**
- **What tangible knowledge, skills, and abilities are you developing, which will help you in the future?**

This chapter will help you explore the answers to these questions. But first, why do you need to answer them at all? **Why isn't it enough to get a college degree and to get a job?**

Before I answer that, I should note that we—the experienced, older adults out here in the world—are the ones who have created this situation. Education is important, even critical, I would argue, to your future success in this world. Indeed, increasingly we live in a world where it is no longer sufficient to have a bachelor's degree; so if for no other reason than credentialing alone, at some point you should start thinking about when you will be going back to school. Education in general, and higher education in particular, opens doors, creates networks, and imparts habits of mind that are fundamental to your future success.

At the same time, there is nothing about the formal educational structure as it currently is configured that prepares you for the working world. Each semester, students are given a list of criteria by which they will be successful: learn this information, read these texts, pass these exams, write these papers, and this is exactly how you will get an "A." Feedback is close to immediate. And at the end of the semester there is a reset; the following semester students get to start again with a new set of courses and expectations.

Presumably, over time, one set of courses prepares you for the next, so you learn how to write an academic paper, how to pass an academic exam, and how to prove your knowledge to those who are assessing it. The culmination of all of this education is a degree; a piece of paper that indicates that *the system we as educated people have created* credentials for you as an educated person.

Like many other traditional systems, the higher-education system has been created to self-perpetuate. Academics are in the business of creating more academics; if they got out of that business they would cease to exist and lose a good bit of their personal and professional identities. Learning how to write and think like an academic is excellent preparation to become an academic.

However, it's not necessarily great preparation to do other sorts of work. Don't get me wrong: I'm not arguing against education as a necessary starting place for many of the careers that exist out there (not to mention the multiples that have not even been created yet). Because, at the end of the day, a great education does teach you how to write, and to think, and to synthesize information, and to criticize and analyze and explore diverse points of view, all of which are necessary for professional and personal success.

But if we couple the current prescribed academic structure with a generation of young people who have been over resourced and cushioned from failing and "taught to the test," then there is little wonder there is a disconnect between expectations and reality for today's young adults.

Take Alexa, for example, the young professional from the beginning of this chapter who is struggling to find fulfillment (not to mention paying her bills) from her "glamorous" magazine job. Alexa was a decent student, president of her sorority, and did two summer internships, one of which at her dad's company. She has never experienced anything anyone would describe as failure, and had pretty lofty expectations for moving quickly up through the ranks in her first professional position. But two years into the job she is discovering that the "real world" doesn't work the way that school did, and just because she wants additional responsibility does not mean it is going to be provided for her.

Study after study finds significant dissatisfaction from employers with college graduates' preparedness for work across items like working with others in teams, ethical judgment and decision making, organizing and evaluating information, oral and written communication, critical and analytical thinking, analyzing and solving complex problems, self-management and resilience, intercultural awareness, and applying knowledge and skills to the real world.[4] One could add to this list that today's college graduates lack an understanding of the complexities and daily realities of how work gets done.

One could make the argument that this disparity is higher education's fault, or that it's the employers' responsibility to bring their new employees up to speed. Ultimately, though, the responsibility falls on you to figure out what you need to be successful and how to get it, whether through traditional education, online, direct experience, or elsewhere.

There are eighty million people in the millennial generation, those born roughly between 1980 and 1994. Unlike previous generations, these young people (who now comprise both entry-level and middle-management positions) don't expect to stick with just one employer for the duration of their careers, although the often-stated perception of the "job-hopping millennial" is turning out to be less true than previously thought.[5] That being said, a recent study by Deloitte across twenty-nine countries found that by 2020, less than three years from now, two-thirds of millennials expect to leave their current employer in order to find greater developmental, leadership, and growth opportunities.[6]

What does this mean for you? It means you can expect to take ownership for your career path; no one is necessarily going to do it for you. And, it means you are competing with a lot of other people for your next opportunity. It's *not enough* just to get a college degree and to get that first job. You also need to think about the following:

- Who are you and what matters to you?
- How can you own your career development?
- How can you intentionally build your skill set from day one?
- How can you claim your space and voice?

Over the next few pages, we will look at each one of these questions and think about how you can use them to **do the work** and own your career.

Identify Your Values

Before you can ever think about what might come next for you, you need to gain some clarity on who you are and what matters to you. **This**

is a question about values, both individual and organizational. There are many things that influence your values—where you were born, your relationships, and your experiences are just a few examples—and much of your young adult lives is a process of gaining more and more clarity about what these things are and how they impact your decision making. Every personal and professional experience you have will provide you with a little more information about the things that you value the most.

Individuals aren't alone in having a set of core values. Every organization has its own set of values, whether its leadership recognizes them or not. Sometimes these values (or guiding principles, or core beliefs) are very explicitly stated and can be found on a website or hanging on the wall or stated in an annual report. These stated values are often better described as "aspirational values," the type of workplace the organization *wants* to create, but may not be reflective of the true day-to-day working practices of a place.

For example, it's all well and good to say "we are an organization that values collaborative thinking," but if you look around and everyone is working alone at their desks with headphones on to drown out the noise of their coworkers, this statement probably is not a true reflection of the actual work culture. What leaders often forget is organizations are made up of people; therefore, the culture of organizations will be created both by the interactions between and the shared values of the people who work there.

The easiest way to change the culture of an organization? Change the people. And changing people is not such an easy thing to do.

In short, you alone probably aren't going to change the values of the place where you work, at least not at this point in your career. What you should do now, is to start reflecting upon what your *individual* values are, and then notice how these align (or don't align) with the place where you work. This sounds like a simple process but it can be rather challenging when you get started. How does one state, in a clear and concise way, *I believe in this but not that?*

One way to think about it is to recognize what are your "nonnegotiables," those things you will not give up, no matter what happens. Or, to put it another way, what are those things for which you would be willing to walk away from your job, if they were threatened?

To start this practice, first look at the list of values in the following list. Is there anything from this list that is missing that you would add? If so, write it in.

Authenticity	Influence
Achievement	Integrity
Adventure	Justice
Authority	Kindness
Autonomy	Knowledge
Balance	Leadership
Compassion	Learning
Challenge	Love
Collaboration	Loyalty
Community	Peace
Competency	Recognition
Creativity	Reputation
Curiosity	Respect
Diversity	Responsibility
Fairness	Risk
Faith	Security
Fame	Service
Family	Spirituality
Freedom	Stability
Fun	Success
Growth	Status
Happiness	Teamwork
Honesty	Trustworthiness
Humor	Wealth
Individuality	Wisdom

Now, **write down your top five personal values or non-negotiables** in the spaces following. If you would like, you can add a short descriptor by each, which defines what the value or nonnegotiable means to you.

_____

_____

_____

_____

_____

You may find that a few of these values change over time, based on your experiences and relationships. For example, when you are younger and have fewer responsibilities, *freedom* and *adventure* might rank high on your list. Later in life, when you have started a family and acquired a mortgage and other possessions, *stability* and *security* could take more prominent positions. **There are no right or wrong answers here**. It's all about what *you* value, what you want to make room for in your life, and what you will use as guideposts to make decisions.

Take some time with this. It may strike you at first as a bit silly, but trust me: this is one of the most important reflective exercises you can do. Indeed, a recent meta-analysis of research studies on college students found that the ability to articulate one's personal values and goals as one of the three key characteristics for long-term success (the other two being cultivating a sense of belonging and a growth mind-set, each of which will be discussed in future chapters).[7] You will be using your list of personal values throughout this book as you assess different life and career decisions; indeed, it's the very foundation of who you are and will and should impact every decision you make.

Once you have some clarity on your own personal values, take a moment to think about the place where you work. Is there a set of stated values? Do you know what they are? Do they reflect the **actual lived values** of the organization? Take another look at the list above.

What are the top five *actual* (nonaspirational) values of your organization? Another way to think about this: What gets measured and held up as "success"?

_____

_____

_____

_____

_____

Now compare your own personal values with the actual values of your organization. How aligned are these two lists? It's not necessary that the two lists are in perfect alignment. And, you may find that while there are different words, similar themes pop up. For example you might have "growth" on your list while your organization values "continual improvement." You may not define those two things in exactly the same way, but the overall theme of personal development may be similar.

You should recognize that the things your organization values are, generally speaking, the things that get rewarded, and what it might mean for you. So, if you are someone who values individuality and your organization values collaboration and teamwork, you need to think about whether you can be more of a team player than an individual contributor in order to be successful there.

Take some time to reflect on the following questions in the space below. **What does the comparison of your values with those of your organization mean for you?**

Is your organization a place that allows you to live out your personal values on a consistent basis?

In what specific ways do you need to modify your behavior in order to be successful?

How do you feel about that?

Again, there are no right or wrong answers here. If you can, find someone who is a mentor or trusted friend to share your responses and your thought process for additional guidance and feedback.

Own Your Career Development

Identifying your personal values and the values of your organization is the first key step in taking ownership for your career development. Indeed, the reality of today's workplace is no one is going to do this for you, so if you're not owning your path, you can expect to stall out.

A major difference between college and life after college in the so-called real world is the extent of autonomy and control you have over what you do. To put it simply, the great joy of being an adult is that there is literally nothing you have to do. There is no job you have to work, no people whom you have to spend time with, or no place where you have to live.

Now, that doesn't mean your choices aren't without consequences; indeed, every choice you make from here on is fraught with consequences, both positive and negative. If you choose to stop showing up to work, you may have more control over your time, *and* you will get fired. If you choose to move to a place where you know no one, you may have a harder time meeting new people, *and* you may vastly expand and diversify your network.

As you can see, the great challenge of being an adult is also that there is literally nothing you have to do. While a lot of people, from relatives to coworkers to friends will no doubt have a lot of opinions on your next moves and the choices and decisions you make, ultimately *you* have to make the decision. From here on, it's all up to you, which can be paralyzing for some.

There are no syllabi or rubrics for life. No one is going to tell you how to get an "A" in your career or life plan, because no such thing exists (more on those plans in a moment). And while you can (and should) look to others for role models and find mentors who can give you feedback and guidance, no one can really tell you what the "right" next move is to ensure a successful and happy life, because no such thing exists. It's a bummer, I know. But it's the honest truth.

So what, then, do you do?

It's time to take ownership for your career development. The hard reality is this: *no one is ever going to care as much about your life and your career as you.* My sincere hope is for many wonderful mentors to step into your life over the years, to provide guidance and wisdom, and to invest in you personally and professionally. But even these people will never care as much about your life and your career as you will. Nor should they!

First, people are too busy caring about their own lives and careers to worry about yours. And second, if you're not willing to care about you, then why should anyone else? You need to demonstrate to other people that you are invested in your own growth and development and that you own the choices and decisions you are making (and the associated consequences), before you can ever ask someone else to help you.

Some of you will read into this as me saying there are "right" or "wrong" choices, that there is a "right" and "wrong" career or life path; for instance, that working on Wall Street is "success" while working as a coffee barista is "failure." Let me be very clear: *This is not what I am saying.* If working as a coffee barista is helping you pay the bills while you pursue your dreams on Broadway, or helping you go back to school, or helping you learn a new trade or skill, and you can own your choice, great. If working on Wall Street aligns with your values, skills, and interests and gives you energy and you can own your choice, great.

But if you're working as a barista as an avoidance tactic or if you're working on Wall Street because it's what someone else told you that you should do, then I recommend you spend some time reconsidering those decisions. Neither, I think you will find, will be sustainable long-term.

So, how do you take ownership for your career development, especially when you are just starting out and feel like you have little ability to own anything?

One strategy I particularly like comes from work on "Intelligent Careers." This theory came out of research in the early 1990s, well before we were talking about millennials and their willingness to move from job to job to build their skill sets (and giving further credence to the notion that this is not just a millennial characteristic). The researchers noted then that traditional career paths were going away in favor of what they called "boundaryless careers"; careers that are defined by the individual over the course of multiple jobs and organizations, as opposed to a single track up a path defined by a single organization. This work identified three critical competencies that can be used to manage one's career, whatever your professional standing or experience level: Knowing Why, Knowing How, and Knowing Whom.[8]

Knowing Why: This career competency is about your ability to articulate what motivates you to do what you do each day. Why did you choose to do this particular job? What motivates you to do your best each day? If your current role or organization does not provide that, what would motivate you in an "ideal state"? Look back at the personal values you identified in the previous section to help guide your response.

Write your answer to the Knowing Why questions here:

Knowing How: This career competency is about the skills and knowledge you need to perform your current role, and, ultimately, the skills and knowledge you will need to successfully move into your next role. To find out about yourself, you need to answer the following questions:

- What do you need to know/be able to do to be successful in your current role?
- What's missing, and how can you obtain those things?
- What will you need to know/be able to do to get to the next role?
- What's missing, and how can you obtain those things?

This presumes, of course, that you know what that next role will be, which you may not. That's OK! But there's value in thinking about what it *could* be. Take a look around at your current organization. What would be a logical next step for you there? What skills, experiences, or knowledge do you need to acquire to move to that next step? What about positions or organizations that are external to your current role? Where are your gaps, and how could you fill them? Remember, "gaps" can come in many forms: certifications, formal education, additional responsibilities or experiences, and so on.

Write your answers, as much as you can, to the Knowing How questions here:

Knowing Whom: Finally, this career competency is about the relationships and people in your network who can both help inform your responses to the Knowing Why and Knowing How questions and provide opportunities and resources to help you fill those gaps. These are the mentors and sponsors whom you already know or whom you need to seek out and add to your existing network. Who do you currently know with whom you can discuss your Knowing Why and Knowing How competencies? Who's missing?

So, great. Now you might be thinking, *You know what? I'm motivated to show up to this job every day because it's paying my bills; a trained monkey could do this job with its eyes closed; and the only people I know are my tyrant of a boss, the barista at the local coffee shop who serves me my iced lattes when I can afford them, and my friends, who are no better equipped to help "support my goals" than I am. Now what?*

It's a fair point. These first few years after college can feel like a slog, sometimes, with no end in sight. It can often leave you asking more questions than finding answers, and one of those questions probably is, *I went to college for this?* And to that I would say, yes, in fact, you did. But that doesn't have to be the end of that story.

Let's return to Alexa, from the beginning of this chapter. Remember Alexa? Alexa is struggling as a sales assistant for a national magazine in New York and questioning why she's working so hard to get seemingly nowhere.

Alexa thought about these questions, too, and came up with the following answers:

Knowing Why: What motivates me, or what would motivate me?

Achievement—feeling like I'm moving forward in my career.

Balance and Fun—these two go together, because I don't feel like I have any balance in my life, and I'm not having much fun, either at work or outside of it.

Creativity—I had a lot of creative outlets in college and I realize now how important it is to me. Nothing about this job feels very creative to me.

Growth—this probably goes with achievement, but I want to feel like I'm building skills and learning new things, and I don't anymore. I want to feel like the people I work for support my growth and development.

Knowing How: What do you need to know/be able to do to be successful in your current role? What's missing, and how can you obtain those things?

Honestly, I feel like I could do this job with my eyes closed at this point. I have to manage some spreadsheets and maintain relationships with clients on a couple of big accounts. Make sure they're happy. Basically I just do whatever my manager tells me to do.

What will you need to know/be able to do to get to the next role? What's missing, and how can you obtain those things?

Six months ago I would have told you I needed additional responsibility on some bigger accounts, and the freedom to manage my own work, so I could eventually get promoted here at this magazine. But now I've realized there really isn't a future for me here. I've asked for more responsibility and I've been turned down every time. I need to be in an environment that supports my growth and development, where it feels like people want me to grow. I need to be somewhere that feels like I'm building a career, not just doing a job. And I don't see myself building a career in the magazine industry. If I'm being honest, I'm not sure if I see myself building a career in New York.

The problem is, I don't know exactly what that career looks like. I actually think I like sales and marketing and would enjoy doing that for something I believed in more; something that allowed me to feel like I was being creative. I never thought I would be in New York long term, and recently I've been thinking more and more about going home to Atlanta. I miss my family and my friends there, and there's so much about that town I love. I always figured I would end up back there, eventually, so why put it off? Maybe I'll stay there forever, maybe not, but what's wrong with going there now?

Knowing Whom: Who do you currently know with whom you can discuss your Knowing Why and Knowing How competencies? Who's missing?

Well, I can't talk to anyone at work about this, and New York is such a small town, there really are very few people here I could talk to without it getting back to my boss. But I've been talking to my dad and he's going to introduce me to some people in Atlanta the next time I'm home, just for some informational interviews. And I'm going to reach out to my former manager at the hospital where I interned during college. I have a mentor from college I'm going to e-mail, too. He's always had great insight on my strengths and interests, and I know he will give me honest feedback on whether or not I'm thinking about this the right way.

As you can see, Alexa doesn't have it all figured out, either, and that's OK. But by taking some time to really reflect on where she is now, and where she might want to be, she has the beginnings of a plan of action she can move forward on. Right now, she doesn't have all of the information she needs to make an informed decision. She needs to have some additional conversations, with family, with former colleagues, with mentors, and with folks she has not yet met to add some insight into what she is thinking.

Alexa needs to think about whether a move back to Atlanta is the right next step for her, and if so, what might that look like? What would she need to make that happen? How will she extricate herself from her life in New York and start to create one in Atlanta? How might the future she is envisioning better align with her values than where she is now? Alexa needs to gather more data, and then she needs to set some goals.

What do I mean by data? Everything is data—all of your experience, relationships, conversations, and research—it all provides critical information and insight, which can and will inform your next steps. Alexa has a little bit of data: she knows what she does and doesn't like about her current role. But she needs to do some research on the job market in Atlanta, the cost of living there, moving costs from Atlanta to New York, and so forth. All of this data, this additional information, will help her make a more informed decision about what might be next, and how to get there from where she is now.

Set One-Year (not Twenty-Year) Goals

This brings us to our next topic, which is all about goal setting. In my work with students and young professionals, I often come across two opposite, yet connected, issues when it comes to goal setting: either the individual is too focused on the long-range or he or she is too worried about being "boxed in" by concrete plans. Both concerns are completely understandable, and both can be paralyzing to forward movement. Let's look at each in turn.

First is **the issue of the long-range plan**. Anyone who knows me will tell you I am a planner. I have to-do lists for my weekends. I love the feeling of checking things off, the satisfaction that comes with knowing I have achieved what I set out to do. At the end of each day, before I leave to go home, I make a list of the things that have to happen the next day, the things I should spend any available time working on, and the longer-range projects that need action but not necessarily immediately. I find this daily practice ensures I am able to "get to work" sooner the next day, without wandering around wondering what I should be working on. (Not surprisingly, I'm a pretty strong "J" on the Myers-Briggs.)

Similarly, I am a strong advocate of setting career and life goals for ourselves. I believe this gives us motivation, it forces us to be intentional about our limited resources of time and energy, and it propels us forward in life in positive ways.

But goals also have a way of setting us up for failure if we do not go about them in the right way. A twenty-year "plan" or "goal" is neither of those things. There are a million different things that are going to happen to you over the next twenty years you cannot possibly envision right now, which will knock you off your plan. You are going to meet someone who turns your whole world upside down. You are going to take a trip someplace you've never been, completely fall in love with that place, and decide to move there. You will discover passions and skills you never knew you had, be dealt some kind of catastrophic life event (let's hope not, but it can happen), lose your life savings gambling in Vegas, or win the lottery.

You get my point. This is the stuff of *life*, the stuff you can't necessarily fully plan for, the stuff that absolutely can and will impact the trajectory and direction of your life.

So, by all means, set a long-range *vision* for your life, identify where you think you want to be in twenty years, and what type of life you want to be living. By doing so, you give yourself an aspiration to work toward, *and* you leave yourself open to course corrections over time, as new relationships and new experiences shift your short-term goals and plans.

Think of your long-range vision as the destination: In twenty years I would like to be living in the Pacific Northwest. The shorter-range goals are the directions: Will you drive or fly? What will you take with you? What will you leave behind? Where will you stop off along the way? What are you going to do when you get there? The other issue with the long-range goal is you never get to celebrate your success, which often can lead to apathy along the way. If you have to wait twenty years to celebrate moving to the Pacific Northwest, at some point you're going to lose your enthusiasm for it.

Fine, you say, then **why set any goals at all?** Why not just go where the wind takes us, and be surprised with where we may end up? (You strong "P" people on the Myers-Briggs will be nodding your heads right about now.) Sure, that's always an option, and sometimes fun things can happen when we stay completely open to the possibilities. Instead of the Pacific Northwest you end up in Colorado, and you think, well, I've always sort of wanted to go to Colorado. And as long as you're happy with that, and feel like you are living a meaningful life according to how you define it, that's just fine.

But sometimes going where the wind takes us ends up looking like stalling. Or we end up in Colorado and realize we hate the snow. Or, we end up twenty years into a career we never intended to pursue, simply because instead of taking ownership for our lives, we let other people dictate where we should go next. Or, the wind may blow an opportunity our way, like a promotion or a move, and we're not in a position to take advantage of it, because we haven't acquired the skills, or the education, or the financial resources that are needed to do so, which we could have been acquiring with just a little forward thinking.

My encouragement to you, then, is to **be intentional,** plan the things you can, **and be open** to the opportunities that present themselves along the way. Set short-term goals—no more than one year at a time—and you won't feel quite so boxed in along the journey. And, you will give yourself the opportunity to celebrate all of your successes along the way. Another benefit to the practice of writing goals is that it is something you likely will have to do for the rest of your professional life. So, you can think of it as skill development, too. Bonus!

A great model to use when writing goal statements is the SMART goal model. Goal statements should be as follows:

Specific and action-oriented: What, specifically, are you going to do?

Measurable: How will you know when you are successful?

Achievable: Does the goal stretch you? Are you setting yourself up for failure?

Realistic: What resources (time, money, people, etc.) will you need to achieve the goal?

Time-bound: When, specifically, will you successfully complete the goal?

A sample SMART goal statement for Alexa might be the following:

Identify three to five sales and marketing opportunities that align with my skills and experience in the Atlanta area by the end of summer.

Now it's your turn. Take a look back at what you wrote under the Knowing Why, Knowing How, and Knowing Whom questions. What do you need to work on? Where are your gaps?

Take some time to **write two to three goals for yourself to address those gaps** over the next year in the space below.

Your goals should be all about what *you* are going to do and not what you want other people to do for you. Look back over your goal statements and make sure these are actions you can and will follow through on implementing. This doesn't mean you may not need other people to help you accomplish your goals, to support you, to provide resources, and to connect you to opportunities. **No one can be successful in a vacuum.** But you are the one who has to do the work.

And, you need to develop a plan to keep yourself accountable to following through and accomplishing these goals. **Find an accountability**

partner: someone with whom you will share your goals and who will periodically ask you how you are doing on them. Set up a regular check-in schedule. Tell them that once a week or month you would like to send them an e-mail to let them know your progress on working toward your goals.

Write down the name of your accountability partner here:

If you can't find an accountability partner, then set a reminder in your calendar with a question to yourself: "What progress have you made on your personal and professional goals?" Hold yourself accountable to the things you said you would do.

Build Your Skill Set from Day One

While you are working on your goals and thinking about the next steps, you can't ignore your current role and responsibilities. As the title of this chapter says, **you have to do the work**, and that doesn't just mean working on figuring out what comes next. Indeed, you're not going to get very far if you don't first focus on being successful where you are.

The first few years in a new position, particularly when you are right out of college, can seem overwhelming and, at times, frustrating. You may find yourself at the bottom of the hierarchy, tasked with less-than-interesting work. You may struggle to navigate the organizational politics and at times feel like you don't belong. You may find yourself saying things like, "I worked my behind off to go to a great college and to graduate with a degree. I deserve better than this!" All of these are perfectly normal feelings.

But here's the thing: the first job was *never* supposed to be the dream job. Can you imagine if it was? Great, you achieved all of your dreams and goals at twenty-two. It's all downhill from here.

I'm joking, sort of, but the reality is that the first job won't be the last job you ever have. Instead, think of it as your opportunity to explore, to build skills, to discover strengths and interests, to build great professional habits, to learn, and to build connections. Remember, *you* have to take ownership for your career and your life. And it starts on the first day in the first job. It all starts by doing the work.

I have a colleague who likes to say to new employees, "If I ask you to sharpen pencils by hand all day, you better be the best pencil sharpener that ever existed." What does she mean by this? Why should she trust someone with the big projects and tasks, and give him or her more responsibility and ownership for work, if he or she can't demonstrate an ability or willingness to knock the small projects and tasks out of the park?

This is the attitude you should bring to your work, every single day. No task is too big or too small. It may feel like some projects are beneath you and beneath that great college degree you just earned. But you know what? *All you have is a college degree.* There are a lot of folks out there with college degrees who would love to have your job. And just because you are an expert at being a college student, it doesn't make you an expert at doing work. In fact, none of us are experts at that, we're all learning as we go. An attitude of learning, humility, and gratitude will take you far.

One of the biggest mistakes I see young people make in their first professional positions is that they forget they are no longer the smartest persons in the room. They forget to be humble and grateful, and they won't acknowledge that they still have a great deal to learn. So here are **ten things to think about** doing in these first few years as a working professional (if not in the years after that, as well):

1. **Accept that you don't know everything (if anything).** Your first few months in any new position are all about you learning how to be a competent, responsible professional in that environment. You will make mistakes. You will learn things about the organization and about work you never knew before. Be a sponge and look for learning moments everywhere you can. Privilege "learning" over "knowing."

2. **Be accountable.** Set and hold high standards for yourself. Do what you say you will do, go above and beyond, and constantly think about what you want people to say about you, after you no longer work there. Focus on the long-term payoffs versus short-term wins. Consistently practice gratitude and humility. Learn the difference between humility—lack of arrogance—and modesty—lack of confidence.

3. **Set goals for your own growth and development.** Take ownership for your own path. What do you need to learn about your organization and industry, and what are the two to three resources you can incorporate into your daily life to gain that knowledge? What are the two to three skills you can develop over the next year through your work? What do you want to be known for in your office? What would you like to see on your résumé in one year, which currently is not there?

4. **Seek out meaningful experiences (but understand that not everything will be a meaningful experience).** You will have the opportunity to speak up and ask for assignments that connect to your goals, and you should. The answer may not always be "yes," but it is always OK to voice your interests. But it's also important to recognize that everyone makes copies and everyone makes coffee. Just because a task doesn't feel "meaningful" doesn't mean it's not valuable.

5. **Seek out opportunities that go beyond (but connect to) the scope of work.** Take advantage of all of the opportunities that come your way. Go hear guest speakers, volunteer for assignments, ask deep questions of yourself and others, take the opportunity to meet people all across the organization, and so on. If you have a mentor or someone you seek out for advice, talk to that person about what you're learning.

6. **Reflect upon your experiences.** Constantly ask yourself open-ended questions such as: What happened? What helped/hindered my success? What would I do differently next time? What did I

learn and how will I apply that in the future? Share your thoughts with your mentor and ask for their reflections as well, both on your experiences and their own.

7. **Seek out feedback and the wisdom of others.** Proactively ask for feedback, both from your mentor and from others. Help others to give you supportive feedback by asking, "On that project we just finished, what are the two to three things you think I did well, and the one to two areas where I could improve?" Pay attention to the process. How you feel during these feedback conversations is as instructive as what you are hearing.

8. **Ask for help.** It is always OK to ask for help. No one expects you to be an expert from day one. Use your mentors, your supervisor, and your colleagues as trusted sounding boards and wise counselors. Though people may seem busy, they would much prefer you to stop and ask for guidance *before* you do something than to ask for forgiveness later. But, pay attention to the answer. You should not need to ask the same question multiple times. And, *before* you ask for help, try to find the answer on your own, first. There's a big difference between asking for guidance on how to effectively meet your goals to your supervisor's expectations, and constantly asking someone to tell you the answer to questions you can easily find with a Google search.

9. **Listen and learn.** This is a biggie. For the first few months, in particular, listen more than you talk. Pay attention to who is talking, and why. Whose voices are privileged in the room? You don't always have to have the "right" answer to everything. Pay attention to diverse points of view, and if you can't find those, seek them out.

10. **Do the work.** Everything starts and ends with the work. You can be the nicest, most fun, most supportive colleague ever, and if your work isn't great, no one is really going to care about how nice and fun you are. Instead they'll say, "He or she's nice, but he or she never meets his or her deadlines." Or, "He or she's fun, but he or she's not really interested in doing the work." Everything that

comes after that "but" is what people will pay attention to. Work hard. Do your absolute best on everything you do. Privilege quality over speed. Be the best pencil sharpener anyone has ever seen.

It's easy when we are working in a job that is less than our dream job to slack off, to not put in our best effort, to do the bare minimum to succeed, because that may be all that is expected of us and that may be all we care about doing. *Do not make this mistake.* Remember those multiple jobs you are going to have over the course of a lifetime? Well, one leads to the next. To get to the great job, which better aligns with your interests and values, you have to do great work in the job you're in now.

Have you ever heard the saying, "Dress for the job you want, not the one you have?" What this means is, you have to give people the impression you can fill that next role, or they will never see you there, and will never give you that opportunity. Well, you need to work for the job you want, not (just) the one you have, too. Be the person who shows up early and stays late, who seeks out additional work when times are slow, who asks colleagues how you can be helpful, who thinks strategically about the work and the organization and looks for opportunities to improve. Demonstrate you're a continual learner by asking for feedback. Go above and beyond to meet if not exceed expectations, and always do what you say you're going to do.

The bottom line is this: **it all begins and ends with the work.** Yes, relationships matter (more on that later), but you can be the most charming person in the world and that alone will not mask if you are constantly letting people down with your work. So think about how you want people to talk about you after you're gone. Think about the kind of recommendation you would like for them to give for you when you are seeking out job number two, or three, or four. Work to be that person. And then you may find the next job actually finds you.

Claim Your Space and Your Voice

Tip number nine, above, notes that at first you should listen a lot more than you talk. One of the biggest struggles I see with young professionals is knowing how, and when, to claim your space and your voice within an organization that may not support you doing so.

One of the key differences between the messages you hear before graduation and after has to do with voice. Before graduation, we tell you your voice matters, and we want to hear it. College is all about learning to think critically, to disagree and express dissent, and to lend your voice to the discussion. After college, in the "real world," these aren't behaviors that necessarily are valued. *You don't know enough yet to have a voice*, you will be told in big and small ways.

Misreading these cues is one of the biggest ways you can trip yourself up in your first professional years. Have a voice, yes. No one is interested in you being a robot or a sheep; indeed, never speaking up can be perceived as disinterest or lack of engagement. But use your voice judiciously. In the beginning, spend more time asking questions than sharing your opinions.

I once worked with a young woman, Erin, who spent the first few months in her new role critiquing and poking holes in her older colleagues' ideas and work. Her criticisms weren't off the mark; indeed, there was a lot of truth to what she was saying. The problem was, she did not yet have the organizational capital to spend in that way. No one was interested in taking critical feedback from the newest, youngest member of the team. And soon enough, her colleagues not only stopped listening to her, they stopped letting her into the room entirely.

You have to learn to read the room. You have to learn to play the politics.

Organizations are made up of people. Organizational culture is created through the lived experiences of the people who work there. And that, inevitably, will have an impact on your ability to be successful and happy in your role. In your first few years, you will learn a lot about the people with whom you work, and the behaviors that are rewarded and privileged.

Before you make assumptions, take some time to listen to and observe the people around you. Pay attention to who gets to speak and who doesn't, who gets rewarded and who doesn't, and how the game of politics is played. If you can find a trusted friend or mentor who can help you navigate and interpret these sometimes treacherous waters, all the better.

Take some time to observe the people who seem to have things figured out.

You will learn over time it's not always fair. Unlike when you were in school and grades were awarded based on merit, aptitude, and hard work, the real world doesn't always work that way. It's lovely when it does, and can be excessively disappointing when it does not. You will find that sometimes people who are not inherently good at their jobs get promoted. Sometimes unethical people get rewarded and are held up as models of success. Sometimes people lacking in leadership abilities are placed into leadership roles and given responsibility for other people's work and lives.

Is it right? No. Is it fair? No. *It just is.* You either have to learn to work within the system, find ways you are able to change the system, or make the choice to leave.

How, then, can you claim your space and your voice within the organizational culture? It bears repeating that everything begins and ends with the work. Do great work; be someone who can be counted on; and treat other people well. If you make a mistake, own it, fix it, apologize, and learn from it. Do your homework and make sure when you do speak up that you are voicing facts based on data and not just opinions. Do the work of learning your own strengths and skills, and ask for greater responsibility on projects that align with those. When someone asks you to work on something that is outside of your current skill set, say yes and use it as an opportunity to learn and to get better. Better yet, step up and volunteer before someone has to ask you.

These aren't magical prescriptions to make everyone play nice together in the sandbox. Whether it's now or later, there will come a time when you are treated unfairly; when you are passed over for a promotion for a far less qualified coworker; when you are silenced in a meeting by a colleague or supervisor; or when, no matter how hard you work, you aren't given the respect you feel you deserve. It will happen. It's inevitable. And you aren't going to be able to prevent it from happening because you can't change other people.

What you do have control over is how you react to these situations. Do you go over your supervisor's head and demand the promotion be given to you? Do you interrupt the person who just silenced you and demand you be allowed your say? Do you demand respect?

These are very personal decisions. As I stated previously, every decision you make has consequences, and it's up to you to gather the data you need, weigh the possible consequences, and then make the decision you feel is right and own it. For example, it's possible that going to management and making the case for why you deserve the promotion over your coworker will result in career advancement for you. It also may damage relationships and put you in a less-secure position down the road. Speaking up in that meeting and defending yourself may earn the respect of colleagues, or it may give you a reputation of being bratty and disrespectful.

Ultimately, **you own your career path**. And that means not only doing great work, but finding a way to speak up and take credit for the great work you have done. It means recognizing when you are being given a great opportunity to build your skills, abilities, and network, and when you are being taken advantage of. It means realizing that sometimes you are too far away from senior management in the organizational hierarchy for them to notice how great you are or how hard you work. There is a fine line between being overconfident and cocky, and being under-confident and meek.

You have to learn to read the organization and know how to play the politics there. This is where mentors, sponsors, and allies become critical not only in helping you learn how to navigate these sometimes dicey waters, but also in speaking up on your behalf. You need people in your corner who have more capital than you do, and who are willing to spend a little bit of it on you. And then, one day when you are in the same position, you need to be willing to spend your capital on those who follow you.

As you grow in your career you will gain the authority and the voice that comes with experience and wisdom. You will gain the capital you need to claim your space, and you will be better able to decide how you want to spend your time. Right now, you need to focus on gaining experience, developing your skills, getting clearer about your personal values, and building relationships. Right now, you need to do the work.

Practice Reflection

1. What has been the most surprising about your first professional experience?

2. What has been the most challenging about your first professional experience?

3. What did you learn about yourself and your organization when you reflected on personal and organizational values?

4. What has been your experience with claiming your space and your voice?

5. How will you use this knowledge about yourself in the next year?

CHAPTER 2: BUILD A LIFE

"If this is being an adult, you can have it back."
— Sarah, Young Professional

Evan grew up in Los Angeles, supported by two highly successful working parents. He graduated from college without any debt and with plans to attend law school after taking some time off to work. During those years between college and law school, he came to a realization, "I've watched my parents, and they work all the time. They have this great big house, and they can't enjoy it. All they do is work. I've realized work-life balance is important to me, and no matter what I plan to create the life I want." He planned to focus on getting a job at one of the smaller law firms that weren't as consumed by billable hours, and he was determined not to get caught up in the prestige chase in law school. But by the winter break of his first year he had forgotten all of those plans. "I've totally given up on that. This is all-consuming. And I'm going after those big firms just like everyone else. Maybe I won't have much of a life. But I can figure that out when I make partner."

I n the first few years after you graduate from college it can be easy to put all of your focus on work (or graduate school, if that's where you find yourself). Without question, work or graduate school will be the single largest occupier of your time and attention. There is no other pursuit that will take up forty-plus hours of your life every week, other than maybe sleep if you're lucky.

And, while it doesn't have to define you or your future, a lot about these first few years of work will set the stage for what comes next. This is when you begin to learn what you do and don't like about work, what your strengths and interests are, and how these things align with your values. It's important that you pay attention, be reflective, and seek out mentors and wise counselors to help you navigate through these critical, early professional experiences.

It's also likely you will put a good deal of focus on the work part of your life during these first few years because that has been your standard operating procedure up until this point. You probably haven't spent a lot of time up until now thinking about things like insurance and retirement planning, health and wellness, and personal growth and development, because you likely have not needed to do so.

Whether it seemed like it or not, up until this point most of your time was largely planned for you and organized around academic calendars. You started school in the fall, took a break for Thanksgiving and the winter holiday, started again in the spring, took a break for spring break, wrapped up in May, and then either traveled, worked, took classes, or did an internship over the summer.

For the past sixteen or so years, your life has been organized by syllabi, and grading rubrics, and every semester you were given the chance to start fresh. You added in some extracurricular activities, hopefully because they were things you were interested in, but mostly, probably, because you thought they looked good on your résumé and would get you to the next step. Occasionally you might go for a run or hit the gym, but that was more of a stress reliever than an intentional focus on long-term health and well-being.

Unfortunately, nothing about your experience up until this moment is great preparation for creating your life, now. Consider the following questions:

- How will you spend your time, now that it is completely your own?
- How do you find and create hobbies?
- What are those individual personal habits—health and wellness, spiritual and emotional, creative—that you value, and how will you prioritize those along with competing priorities of work, family, and social time?
- What happens when things don't go exactly as you had planned and there is no safety net?
- What should you be doing, now, to plan for your future?
- How do you find friends, as an adult?
- How do you maintain old relationships along with new ones?

- How do you find mentors and sponsors?
- How do you get involved in your community in meaningful ways?

It's a lot, right? Don't worry; we'll be working through each of these questions over the next two chapters. These are just a few of the "life" questions you will have to grapple with over the next few years. Remember, the great gift of being an adult is that *you* get to decide how you spend your time and with whom. The great challenge of being an adult is that you do have to decide. (And, to be clear: not making a choice is still making one.)

As the quote at the top of this chapter indicates, these big life decisions can be a burden at times. That quote comes from a young adult named Sarah, several years into balancing graduate school and work and life postcollege, facing the realities of that world versus what she now realizes was her relatively responsibility-free existence as a college student: "If this is being an adult, you can have it back." It's a sentiment you are probably agreeing with right about now.

This chapter explores the first part of that dilemma—how will you spend your time and other valuable limited resources—while the next chapter goes deeper into the issue of building community, both personally and professionally. All of it, together—the work you do, your personal resources, the people you surround yourself with—add up to ensure you are creating the life *you* want.

Define Your Balance

Much like with the job-search process, as you build a life you need to choose to do the things *you* want to do, not what you think others think you should do. Only you get to show up every day and live your life. If you're not paying attention, it can be easy to find yourself months or years down a path that was chosen for you, as opposed to one you chose for yourself. You need to live the life *you* want to live, not the life somebody else should be living. And, you need to remember all choices have consequences, some positive, some negative.

By choosing the big-law-firm route, our friend, Evan, is choosing a higher salary, which will give him the ability to live in a nicer apartment, eat at nicer restaurants, and perhaps go on expensive vacations. However, he is also choosing to work upward of eighty or ninety hours a week in order to earn that higher salary, which means he won't spend a lot of time in that nice apartment, he will eat most of his meals at his desk or on the run between client meetings, and he rarely will have time to take one of those expensive vacations. As he himself says, he'll find a life when he makes partner in eight or ten years. That's the choice he's willing to make, and he's prepared to deal with the consequences.

That's *Evan's* choice. What matters isn't whether or not you or I or anyone else thinks it's the "right" choice, what matters is whether it's the right choice for *him*. Now **you need to figure out what are the right choices for you**. So, just as you're thinking about things like, what type of work do I want to be doing, and what type of organization do I want to be a part of, you also need to think about where you want to be doing that work and how it will fit into the type of life you want to have. Is it important to you to live in a big city? Is it important to you to live somewhere where you have a built-in network? Is it important to you to live close to family or would you rather go to a part of the world where you've never been?

All of these questions and many more can impact the type of work you may end of doing, and where.

For example, I have made the choice to work in education in a relatively low cost-of-living community. I have a good life, a comfortable life, a life that aligns with my values of stability and security and autonomy. There has been a part of me that has always regretted not doing the big-city thing in a place like New York. However, I also know I am not willing to live in a big city on an educator's salary.

While autonomy in my work is of utmost importance to me, I also depend on having health insurance so I don't have to pay for medical bills out of pocket, and being able to contribute to my future through retirement funds. These things align with my values of stability and security. I also know I gain great value from the things I do outside of work, and having the time to pursue them, and there is a part of me that derives meaning from working for a cause that seems bigger than myself.

All of these elements align with my choice to work in education in the place where I do. It's a career that provides reasonable balance between time at work and time for outside-of-work activities; it's a cause I believe in; and it provides me the stability and security I desire, as well as autonomy in my work. Each of these factors has contributed to my choices to work in the field I am working in, in the place where I choose to do it.

A lot has been written about the concept of "work-life balance" in the past few years. From Sheryl Sandberg's *Lean In* to Anne Marie Slaughter's piece in *The Atlantic*, "Why Women Can't Have it All," it seems a lot of folks, mostly women but not exclusively, are starting to question the appropriate balance between building a career and building a life.[9]

And while the articles and books may be written by those in the Gen X or Boomer generations, it's actually the millennials who are making the biggest push for what they are calling "integrated" lives, which allow for a natural flow between work and life. With the rise of social media and smartphones and 24-7 access, this generation is saying, fine, I'll be available to answer e-mails and work on projects while I watch the late-night TV shows, but I'm also going to step away from work to take that yoga class midmorning. Indeed, many millennials say they will leave an organization if it does not allow them to have the sort of work-life balance or flexibility they are seeking.[10]

Whether or not this rings true for you, there are a couple of points I feel are worth noting here. First, you need to recognize where you sit in the organizational hierarchy. Yes, you should pay attention to how the organization aligns or does not align with your personal values. Yes, you should pay attention to the work environment, the work culture, and the people with whom you are working and how those things fit or do not fit with what you want out of a work environment, work culture, and colleagues.

And, you should be mindful of the fact that just because you want something it doesn't mean you're going to get it.

The first few years in any new job are all about hard work, relationship building, and building capital. Again, choices have consequences. If you are looking to do the least amount of work possible to earn a paycheck, you can find those jobs. But you should not at the same time expect high financial rewards or career advancement. I am at a point in my career where I can fairly well dictate the type of work I will or will not do, and the type of organization I would like to be part of while doing it. That was not the case twenty years and two degrees ago, and it likely will not be the case for you, yet, either.

You also need to define what you mean by "balance." That term is laden with assumptions, misperceptions, and judgments. The actual enactment of the term is a very personal and individual thing. For some it means no work at night or on the weekends. For others it means dinner with the family and then going back to work once the kids are in bed. For others it means working long hours for an extended period of time, followed by an intense break. For some it means drawing clear lines between "work" time and "personal" time, while for others those two concepts merge into one.

What's important is what *you* envision a life of balance, or integration, or fulfillment to be, and then figuring out the steps *you* can take (not what you expect others to do for you) to move closer to that envisioned life.

Now is the time to reflect on that. Take some time to write out answers to the questions below:

What does work-life balance (or integration, or fulfillment) mean to you? How do you define or describe that?

In a perfect world, one that looked like what you just described, how would you spend your nonwork time? How structured would that time be?

What's currently stopping you from creating that life for yourself?

What are the one or two steps *you* can take in the next three to six months to move you closer to that imagined life?

Not everything will be within your control, especially when you're just starting out. But this is the time to **start taking the steps you need to take** to create the life you want. Don't wait for someone to do it for you. They won't. They're too busy creating a life of their own.

Manage Your Time

When you enter the adult world of work, at first it seems like you have a lot of freedom. "I can do whatever I want!" you suddenly realize. No one's telling you what to do, or when to do it, or how to do it. No one's telling you to clean your home, or to eat something better than takeout food for every meal, or to go to the gym, or to join a church, or to find a place to volunteer.

And you know what? For a little while, I think that's OK. Enjoy the freedom. Live like a slob. Stay out late and sleep your weekend away. You've worked pretty hard to get to this point, and you're probably realizing that while adult work life comes with a good bit of freedom, it also comes with a good bit of exhaustion. One of the worst things you can do, right out of the gate, is to throw yourself into a thousand different activities to fill every available waking minute. That's pretty much a recipe for disaster. You need to get used to the rhythms of work life, and how it feels to get up day after day and put in a full day's work.

But after you get through a few months of that, you will start to realize how much sleep you really need to be functional at work.[11] And, you will start to realize there are only so many hours available to you outside of work to fit in other activities. While you may have been able to power through on two hours of sleep and join fourteen different organizations and keep up with a double major and two minors in college, that sort of schedule just isn't going to work for very long in your life after college. The stakes only get higher for how you show up, the effort you put in, and the accomplishments you achieve.

Sure, it was possible to fail a class in college, and enough of that would lead to getting kicked out of school. But I'm assuming if you're reading this, you're probably not one of those people. Miss multiple deadlines, show up consistently late and unprepared, sleepwalk through your days and you *will* lose your job, which means losing a paycheck, health insurance, retirement funds, and opportunities to find another position. Often, social networks are intertwined enough that even failing at a volunteer commitment can have serious ramifications. You only have one reputation, and it goes with you everywhere.

You need to do the work, yes. But you also need to manage your time, and to manage it well.

What sort of things do you need to make time for outside of working hours? First are the basics: grocery shopping, laundry, cleaning your house, personal hygiene, making and managing a budget, and paying your bills on time. These range from daily to weekly to monthly activities. They may seem silly—of course you're going to go to the grocery!—but each takes time, which is time you won't spend doing something else.

Friends and family are a second area you need to make time for. Do you talk to your family every day? Is it important to you to connect with friends each week over dinner or coffee or a night out? Do you need to plan time to join groups, which will broaden your friend network? This also may seem like an odd area to budget time for, but you will be surprised how quickly it can overwhelm your schedule. Alternatively, if you don't make time for personal connections, you will soon discover how lonely those hours between work and sleep can become.

Remember: life is a series of choices. Every hour you choose to spend doing one thing is an hour you won't spend doing something else.

The third area consists of extracurricular activities. I've lost count of the number of young adults who have said to me, "How do I find hobbies?" After a few times of hearing it, it struck me what an indicator this question is for this generation's overscheduled experience up until this point. You don't know how to find hobbies because you've never had to, before. They have all been chosen for you, scripted into your life along with tutors and test prep and everything else. But now you're on your own to decide what it is you like to do, and how and where you will find places to do it.

There are several ways of attacking this. First, look back at the extracurricular activities you pursued in college, and see what stands out for you, or what you particularly miss doing. Second, you can find and join a whole bunch of things, committing to let a few drop within six months once you figure out what you really like to do. Or, third, just find and pick one thing. Sign up to volunteer as a tutor on Saturdays. Join a choir. Join a book club. Join a civic organization. Join a local intramural sports league. Go see what it's about. Just because you pick something doesn't mean it has to be a lifetime commitment.

Think back to those personal values you identified. What are your nonnegotiables? How can you identify activities, which fill your available free time, that align with those? For example, if "faith" is one of your top five values, do you need to find a church family to join? Do you need to adopt a regular spiritual practice to guide and shape the decisions and choices you are making?

Finally, don't forget to budget in time just for yourself, too. This will be particularly valuable for you introverts who need some dedicated "downtime" to recharge your batteries. It will be tempting, at first, to fill all of the available free time between working and sleeping with some kind of "constructive" activity. It can be easy to let the "fear of missing out," or FOMO, mind-set dictate your schedule. But we all need time to rest and to be still.[12] No one gets bonus points for running on fumes all the time.

There will always be another dinner, another night out, another party, another whatever it is that is making you feel guilty. Sometimes the best time is that which is spent in quiet.

Take, for example, Elliott, who works in Atlanta in corporate real estate, which is a job that is a perfect fit for his extroverted personality. He spends his days on the go: meeting clients, showing properties, and making deals. He is never without his phone, and always thinking about work. He also enjoys a very active social life, and most nights of the week he is out to dinner, meeting friends for drinks, or attending a party or a sporting event. Even during these "personal" hours, he's constantly thinking about how he is making connections that might benefit him at work. Many days he is operating on just four or five hours of sleep, and he is living on a steady diet of caffeine and carbs.

Finally, he realized, something had to give. He had put on twenty pounds and he started feeling distracted and like he had no energy at work. "I started to dread Mondays, which I've never done. So I made a rule: only one night out on the weekends, and the other night I have to turn my phone off at eight. And I started biking to work. It means a longer commute, but I get in some exercise, and that's thirty minutes twice a day I can't be on my phone and I have to be fully present. I feel so much calmer now. More like my old self."

So, how do you plan for all of these things in the course of a week? Just like you would with your finances (more on that in a moment), start by creating a time budget for yourself.

Take a moment to create a budget like the example following. Start by blocking out work hours, travel to and from work, and the time you need in the morning to get ready. Then, think about how much sleep you would like to get each day, and fill that in. Now you know the available time you have left, and you can start to piece together the activities listed above.

	Sunday	Monday	Tuesday	Wednesday	Thursday	Friday	Saturday
12:00 a.m.							
1:00 a.m.							
2:00 a.m.							
3:00 a.m.							
4:00 a.m.							
5:00 a.m.							
6:00 a.m.							
7:00 a.m.							
8:00 a.m.							
9:00 a.m.							
10:00 a.m.							
11:00 a.m.							
12:00 p.m.							
1:00 p.m.							
2:00 p.m.							
3:00 p.m.							
4:00 p.m.							
5:00 p.m.							
6:00 p.m.							
7:00 p.m.							
8:00 p.m.							
9:00 p.m.							
10:00 p.m.							
11:00 p.m.							

If you find it difficult to project forward, then take this chart and for a week or two make a concerted effort to write down how you currently spend your time. Don't cheat! Be honest with yourself.

At the end of two weeks, reflect on how you are *actually* spending your time. Are there big gaps of unused time? Are there places where you are trying to do too much? Are you perpetually late to work because you aren't giving yourself enough travel time, or are you completely drained by the time Friday gets here because you aren't getting enough sleep? Often, just seeing how we are spending our resources (in this case, time) in writing can open our eyes to waste or excess in ways we could not see clearly, before.

Prioritize Health and Wellness

Another area which will require dedicated time is health and wellness, and it's so important I wanted to put it in its own section. The point of this section is not to be your exercise coach or your physician or your therapist, as I am none of those things. The point is to recognize that those things exist, and you need to value them and seek them out as needed.

It's time to own your life. No one, other than perhaps your mother and your physician, is going to tell you to get enough sleep, to eat well, and to exercise. No one is going to tell you to make sure to make time for your emotional and mental well-being. Why? Because they're too busy worrying about those things for themselves, to worry about whether or not you're doing them. *You* have to take care of yourself. And just like everything else, starting those habits and practices early will pay off huge dividends in the long run.

Think of this as a simple checklist:

1. **Find local doctors.** You're not a kid anymore; it's time to find your own adult medical professionals, no more going to see your pediatrician. Your health needs change as you get older, and your medical professionals should reflect these. At a minimum you should find a general practitioner, a dentist, an eye doctor, a dermatologist, and for women, an ob-gyn.

   If you're not sure where to find them, ask coworkers or friends for recommendations. You can also check with your organization's HR department to see if they recommend certain doctors. Ask about "in-network" versus "out-of-network" providers. In-network providers will be preferred by your health insurance and you will pay less out of your own pocket.

2. **Find a pharmacy.** If you don't take routine prescriptions, finding a local pharmacy you like and trust won't be as critical. But at some point we all get sick and at the very least need some over-the-counter medication. Having a go-to spot *before* this happens will ease your peace of mind. Also, most pharmacies now provide annual flu shots that are covered by health insurance, if this is something you choose to do.

3. **Find an exercise routine.** For some, this will mean researching and finding a local gym that fits your budget. For others, this will

mean joining local intramural sports, running groups, or other organized outdoor activities. You might choose to walk or bike to work each day, or commit to going for a walk or a run after work. It really doesn't matter what it is, just know that most work activities today involve sitting at a desk all day; prolonged sitting has been linked to increased cardiovascular disease, excess insulin production, and increased cancer risk, not to mention muscle degeneration.[13] Imagine, then, what thirty to forty years of that will lead to! So get moving, and make it a part of your regular routine.

4. **Learn to cook.** Eating out all the time isn't just bad for your waistline, it's also bad for your wallet. As much as you can, take time to make your own food at home. Cooking for yourself allows you to make better choices in terms of what goes into your meals, and frankly it's just a skill everyone should have. You don't need to be a master chef, but you should at least know how to boil an egg, cook chicken, and make a pot of spaghetti.

    If you're still craving the social experience of eating out, host potluck suppers. If you need an incentive, each time you choose not to eat out, take the money you would have spent and put it into your savings account. At the end of the month, take stock of how much you have saved and congratulate yourself for making smart choices.

5. **Practice self-care.** The term "self-care" has been a bit overused recently but it's a part of your health and wellness toolkit. There are really three steps to practicing self-care. First, you need to recognize when you need it. You need to have the awareness to notice you are feeling run-down, or off, or a bit unbalanced. Second, you need to be able to self-diagnose. Do you need sleep? Time to yourself? A change in diet? A social-media blackout? Time with friends or a good book? Third, and most importantly, you need to be willing and able to take the step that is needed. Make time for sleep, choose a healthy meal, turn off the computer, take a pause in your day, or do whatever it is you need to do.

And, if things still aren't right, don't hesitate to seek out professional guidance. Just like you would go see a physician if you had the flu, or an emergency-room doctor if you broke your arm, go see a counselor if you need mental or emotional guidance. We all need a "checkup from the neck up" from time to time, as one of my mentors is fond of saying.

Own Your Finances

I'm always a bit surprised by how many young adults have not given much thought to things like retirement planning, health insurance, rainy-day funds, or other long-term planning. Repeatedly, research demonstrates today's young adults are not saving enough for their futures.[14] Listen, I get it. Some of these things seem really far off. Planning for the long-term, sometimes for thirty or more years down the road, is hard to do. It's even harder to do when you're struggling just to pay the rent and bills.

But the reality is, the sooner you start to save now, even if it's just a small amount each month, the better off you will be later. This is the beauty of compounding interest. For now, you may still be covered by your parents' health coverage and have them as a bit of a fallback plan for financial worries. But that won't always be the case. And, as long as you depend upon them for your financial security, and defer to them in your financial decision making, the longer you put off owning your adulthood. It's time to grow up and take ownership for your choices and decisions. And that means taking stock of your present and your future, and starting to make intentional plans for both.

Just like I'm not your doctor or your therapist, it is not my goal here to be your financial adviser. What I do want to do is to encourage you to *get* a financial adviser. Just like with a doctor, find someone you trust, whom you feel you can be completely honest with and will be completely honest with you, and who will help you think about what you should start doing, right now.

Before you take that step, here are some questions to ask yourself:

- Do you need to pay off student loans?
- Do you plan to buy a house in the next five years?
- Do you want to take an annual vacation trip somewhere?

- When do you think you want to retire?
- Do you plan to start a family?
- Will you need to be able to take care of your parents or other family members one day?
- Do you plan to go back to school?
- Do you have credit card or other debt you need to pay off?
- Do you have health issues that will require long-term care?
- Are you currently living within your means?
- Do you have enough saved to cover you for three to six months if you lost your job?

It's also time to start doing short-term planning, if you're not already, which means making a monthly (or a weekly, whatever works for you) budget and sticking to it. Just like you only have twenty-four hours in the day, you only have so much money in the bank each month to spend. Making a budget, and sticking to it, is the way to make sure you live within your means and have money to put toward saving. It will mean making hard choices. But that's what being an adult is about.

Just like you did with your time, create a simple chart to track your current expenses. This time, start by tracking them for a month, and then use the data to create a budget for the next month. Take note of where you're spending money unnecessarily, and where you're being perhaps unnecessarily frugal. By writing everything down, and being completely honest with yourself, you'll become aware of where you are spending too much and where you can put more resources. At the top, list the various categories that make the most sense to you. You might use, for example:

Rent/ Utilities	Grocery/ Eating Out	Coffee	Toiletries	Misc.	Savings

Use what works for you. As you go you may find you need to add a category. Under each category **list each and every expense** you make over the month, and add up the total at the bottom.

After you get a hold on how you are *currently* spending your money, you can then create a spreadsheet, which allocates a budgeted amount to each category each month, and work to stay within those budgeted limits. Should you want an online budgeting tool, check out Mint.com as a resource.

This short-term budgeting and long-term planning also impacts the choices you will make about your career and life. There used to be a rule that you should spend no more than 30 percent of your income on rent (or a mortgage). However, with skyrocketing rents in cities like New York, DC, San Francisco, Boston, and others where many of today's young professionals like to live, the reality is, this is no longer a reasonable expectation.

If you want to live in Washington, DC and you only bring home $2,000 per month, then you either need to find a roommate or be willing to live outside the city where rents are cheaper and commute in (but remember there's a cost to that commute, too). Can you do that and still put away a rainy-day fund in case of emergencies and start saving for retirement? Can you do all of that and take a vacation once a year? Are these things important to you?

Only you can answer those questions, but you need to start asking them.

Redefine "Failure"

It may seem a little odd to wrap up this section about planning and making decisions to talk about embracing failure. But it's actually a critically relevant topic, especially as you are thinking about how you will build a life.

More than any other generation, failure, unfortunately, is just not part of your DNA. As the "trophy generation," you have been protected from failure, surrounded by tutors and teachers and parents and counselors and so many support systems that you have not just been shielded from the perils of failure, you have been taught that failure is not acceptable. And that was most definitely not the lesson you needed to learn.

First of all, let's take a moment to define what is meant by "failure." Due to all of those aforementioned support systems, things that previously would have been defined as a "mistake" or "less than satisfactory" have now risen to the level of "failure." In school, getting an F letter grade is the very definition of failure. Suddenly, anything less than an A or B, in all subjects, is seen as failing.

In work, a legitimate failure might look like starting your own business, not selling any product, and losing all of your investors' money. Failure might look like getting fired for poor performance or stealing from the company (the latter being not just failure but illegal). Failure does *not* look like sending an e-mail you didn't mean to send, or getting a thousand copies made of a promotional flier with a typo on it. Those are mistakes, and they should be corrected, but that's not failing.

A few years ago a young professional named Ann was looking to make a move into the tech industry, and managed to work her connections to get an informational interview with one of the senior leaders at a leading Silicon Valley firm. The call lasted close to an hour, after which she asked if we could debrief the experience. As we talked through it, it became clear she was feeling a great bit of disappointment because there was no job offer made to her at the end of the call, despite the fact that this had been neither the reason for nor the expectation of the conversation.

"I guess what I've learned from this is I need to get used to failure," she said to me.

I was stunned. "That's not failure," I said. "You just had close to an hour-long conversation with one of the top execs at one of the top tech companies in the world. That's a huge success!"

You have to learn to set your expectations appropriately. And, you need to talk with your manager and coworkers about their expectations, too. This is why goal setting is so important. It helps to set realistic targets and defines metrics for success (and failure).

Failure in life, if you're doing it right, is inevitable. That doesn't mean you should strive for it, necessarily, content to live in mediocrity, but if you're not failing at something every once in a while, then you probably haven't set your goals high enough. It's like that old saying, "Aim low, and hit your target every time." There may be a limited amount of satisfaction in that, but not for long. A mistake is not a failure. Deciding we made the wrong choice, and choosing to make another, is not failure. Indeed, I call that success! That's called learning and growing and getting smarter.

In practice, this means never going after the next promotion for fear you might not get it. Not going to the social gathering for fear you might not know anyone. Not raising your hand for the volunteer assignment for fear you might not like it. You know what? You may not. But if you don't try, if you don't show up, if you don't put yourself out there, you most certainly won't. Notice the common word in all of those phrases: "fear." Too often too many of us let our fear of failure prevent us from moving forward.

The positive-psychology researcher Shawn Achor tells us 90 percent of our long-term happiness is predicted *not* by the world around us, but by how our brain processes the world around us.[15] Our obsession with avoiding failure has conditioned our brains to equate mistakes with failure and shame. When you don't know how to be vulnerable, you can't own your mistakes as learning opportunities. As the researcher Brene Brown describes it, we've moved from thinking "I did something bad" (guilt) to "I am bad" (shame).[16] That is an utterly paralyzing place to be, one which will never allow you to move forward in your life in any productive and meaningful way.

I'm often struck by how many young adults living in New York actually don't want to be there. They are looking for someone, anyone, to give them permission to leave. One young woman looked at me and said, "I had to do the New York thing, to prove I could. But I can't be here forever. This isn't the life I want." She could identify that she wasn't where she wanted to be, but she couldn't quite figure out how to leave, as if she would be letting people—her parents, her friends, herself—down if she did. And she couldn't quite figure out what the next step should be. It was almost too overwhelming to contemplate, so she continued to live there, living a life she did not want, waiting for someone to tell her what to do.

Today's young adults are looking for a playbook. "Tell me exactly the right choice to make so I don't screw up the next twenty years of my life," they say to me. Unfortunately, no such thing exists. You are living the playbook, creating it every day. There is no one right choice, and all choices have consequences, both positive and negative. Make your choice, and own it. And once you've done so, if you find you're not living the life you want to live, then it's up to you to make a different choice, to make a change.

You get just this one life. How are you going to live it? What do you want from it? It's time to create the life you want to live.

Practice Reflection

1. What has been particularly challenging for you as you strive to balance (or integrate) work and life?

2. What did you learn about yourself when you made your time budget?

3. What are the two or three steps you can take in the next six months to own your finances?

4. What have you failed at? What did you learn from that experience?

5. How will you use this knowledge about yourself in the next year?

CHAPTER 3: CREATE COMMUNITY

Live Where You Live

Matt was someone who you could say excelled *at college. He was a great student, incredibly popular, involved in and led organizations that made a difference, and well liked by students, faculty, and staff. When he reached his senior year, after doing several summer internships in New York and Chicago, he found himself with multiple job offers. A couple were great professional opportunities—management-development rotational programs with lots of rooms for advancement—while the other two were less great on paper but located in cities with lots of young people, including a lot of his fellow classmates and fraternity brothers. One was in Charlotte, his hometown. He knew he wanted to end up there eventually, but he wasn't sure he was quite ready to go back yet. And, there was something about going to the places where everyone else was going that concerned him. "It would be easy, sure, but I'm not sure easy is what I'm looking for or what I need right now." Instead, he chose one of the rotational programs and was sent to Minneapolis for the first year. Nine months in he found himself living in a one-bedroom apartment and doing some soul-searching about the choice he had made. "I thought I wanted a challenge, but I'm not sure this is it. I'm starting to realize all of my friends live in other cities, and deep, meaningful relationships are important to me. I don't know. Maybe this isn't the town or the job for me."*

Building a life, which was covered in the previous chapter, isn't just a checklist of tasks and to-do items to cross off one at a time. This may have been how you managed life up to this point—go to college, check; join organizations, check; pick a major, check; study abroad, check; find a job, check—but it's not how you should be doing things now. Sure, there are those items, which were discussed previously, like finding doctors, establishing routines, creating financial plans, which are the logistical details of day-to-day existence as a grown-up. But building a life, *actually living*, is so much more than that. Because **building a life is also about building community**, professionally and personally.

As Matt and many others have discovered once they leave college, making friends as a grown-up can be quite challenging. You may have looked forward to establishing new, grown-up relationships as a working adult and idealized deep, meaningful conversations over wine and cheese about politics and literature, but the reality is that those conversations were actually more likely to happen *during* college than outside of it.

During college you were surrounded by like-minded people—yes, perhaps *too* like-minded at times—all of whom were in the same place with similar goals related to educational enrichment. Whether you took advantage of it or not, you were all there to think deep thoughts, to have intellectual discussions and debates, to learn, and to challenge yourselves.

Most people in the real world don't have a lot of time for that. There's a reason we all look nostalgically at our college days, and it's not only about the tailgates and parties! In the real world, we're all doing work to pay the bills, taking out the trash and fixing dinner, taking care of children and significant others and aging parents, and dealing with all of the concerns that come along with those things. It's a luxury to engage in philosophical debate.

That does not mean you should not look for those opportunities, should they hold meaning for you. It just means it's going to take more work to make them happen than you might have anticipated.

Unlike in college, where traditional students are generally between the ages of eighteen to twenty-two or so, once you graduate and start to work you will most likely be the youngest person in the office. If you're lucky you may be in some kind of a cohort program or in graduate school with people your own age. But how do you build a relationship with Diane, the single mother of two teenagers, or Frank, the married father of three kids under the age of ten? You likely will find you don't have a lot in common with these people, and they have a lot of outside commitments to attend to that don't include going to happy hour with you after work.

One thing I think you need to remember as you are navigating through these sometimes uncomfortable waters is that **you have been here**

before. It just did not look the same as it does now. But when you got to college you had to figure out how to find friends, how to find organizations, which aligned with your interests, to join, how to find those wise counselors and mentors who were there to show you the way, and how to build intentional community with friends and significant others.

For a while it might have been unpleasant, and you may have been a bit homesick for your high-school friends, teachers, and the familiarity of your family. You may have felt a bit like an impostor who was let in someplace you didn't belong and wondered why everyone else had it figured out but you (more on that in the next chapter). And then what happened? Little by little, you figured it out and you found your place. So now you're going through the same thing, with a bit of a different look to it.

Remind yourself: **you have all of the tools you need to be successful here, inside you, right now.**

One of the first and best lessons to learn through this is patience. I know! You're thinking, *that's the worst!* And it is. And it's important. In fact, if you can find a way to embrace it, to be comfortable in your aloneness, this can actually be some of the most valuable time you will spend in these first few years.

Our friend Matt from the beginning of this chapter has now been through several rotations in several new cities, and each time, he finds he gets better at it. He now knows how to find friends, how to find "his people," how to find the type of living and cultural and community spaces in which he thrives. And, he shared with me, he's learned, "It takes about six to nine months to really feel like you *live* in a place." That's important. It doesn't happen overnight. For a while you're going to be off your game, off your normal routines and rhythms, feeling like that impostor. And Matt would be the first to tell you in that first stint in Minneapolis he didn't even really try. He didn't *live where he lived*, and it impacted everything about his experience there.

Live Where You Live

"You need to live where you live." I use this phrase a lot. What do I mean by that? Hang pictures on the walls. Join groups. Volunteer for things. Make connections. Explore. Even if you're just there for a one-year rotation, like Matt, or for graduate school with a finite end point, you need to dive in and act like you're going to be there forever.

First of all, you never know what may happen. When I moved to Georgia for graduate school immediately after college, I only planned to be there for two years. Then, after graduating with my master's degree, I took up a job with the university. This was supposed to be a temporary thing until I figured out "what I was really going to do with my life." (Literally, I started there as a two-week temp.)

I signed a three-month lease for one of the cheapest apartments I could find. I didn't hang pictures; I barely unpacked. My "dining table" was a plastic outdoor patio set. Eventually I started attending a church but never joined, talked about how I would like to volunteer as a tutor or a mentor in the schools but never signed up, made some friends but didn't really allow myself deep, meaningful relationships. Why? At any moment I was going to leave, and I didn't want commitments I couldn't separate myself from. *I don't want to let people down*, I told myself. *I'm not actually going to stay here.*

And then what happened? I re-signed that three-month lease, every three months, *for five years*, until I actually bought a home there. By the time I left Georgia, I had been there for fifteen years, had been through two significant relationships, had a master's degree and a doctorate, and frankly could have mentored a child from elementary school all the way to college had I just signed up for it.

You never ever know what is going to happen. You know that old saying? *Life is what happens to you while you're busy making other plans.* Don't get so consumed by the process and the plan that you forget to *live*.

The other reason you need to *live where you live* is that it just is going to make you happier. Make your home a place where you want to be. Hang pictures on the walls, get decent bedding and towels, and go buy some nice dishes. Even if you end up leaving and going somewhere else, these are things you will take with you, so they are good investments. Other than work, your home is the place where you will spend the most time, even if it is only to sleep. You want it to be a place where you like to be.

Now, that does not mean buying out the Pottery Barn catalog and going into massive amounts of debt! Be smart about this. But find ways to make your home a place where you are happy, arguably the place where you are the happiest. Even if things aren't going perfectly at work, especially if things aren't going perfectly at work, then you want your home to be a place where you are happy, feel safe, and feel comfortable.

But it's not just about your home. After all, if all you are doing is sitting at home on your very comfortable couch by yourself night after night, then you're not building much of a life. You also need to think about the relationships in your life, both the ones you already have and how (and if) you will maintain them, and those new relationships you may now choose to cultivate.

As humans, we are inherently social beings.[17] We want to be in community with others. Our lives are enriched by it. As Shawn Achor notes in *The Happiness Advantage*, "when we have a community of people we can count on—spouse, family, friends, colleagues—we multiply our emotional, intellectual, and physical resources. We bounce back from setbacks faster, accomplish more, and feel a greater sense of purpose."[18] There is much to be gained from being in community with others, both personally and professionally.

As an adult, no one is going to force you into relationships or tell you whom to be friends with. Just like the struggle to find hobbies, finding friends—good, real friends who align with your values—can be one of the greatest challenges adults face.

And I would remind you here that **you have been in this place before**. You have had to make friends before. You know how to do this, you just may not remember doing it, because we tend to block out the challenging and difficult times and focus on the happier ones. And, of course, unlike college, you're now lacking some of the social supports like resident hall life and organized social interactions, which forced you into community with others and provided opportunities to meet new people and to make new friends. Now you have to build those things into your life for yourself. You have to take ownership for your life.

One of the most difficult realities to face as an adult is that some of our former friends, the ones who once seemed so important to us, no longer add value to our lives and in fact may be detracting from them. Sometimes people are meant to be with us in certain parts of our journey, but not in all of it. It is perfectly OK to have high-school friends, college friends, graduate-school friends, first job/city friends, and so on and not have those people cross over from one stage to the next. At some point you may find a partner and have children and build relationships with people who are in a similar phase of life.

As we've discussed, you are going to learn very quickly as a working adult that your time is a precious commodity, and you have very little of it. It is just not feasible to maintain all of your former relationships at the same level you once did, or you are going to burn out, and quickly.

Nor does it make much sense. Why *should* you have the same deep relationship with people you used to live with and spend roughly twenty-four hours a day with, now that you live across the country from each other? Which are those few relationships where you are committed to investing your limited time in a meaningful way? And, who are those people who seem willing to invest in you?

We all need both strong and weak ties.[19] Strong ties are those close friends, family members, the people who know you well, who have seen you at your best and your worst, and would do just about anything for you. These are the people who will always answer the phone when you call. But not all of your acquaintances and connections have to be, nor should they be, close friends and strong ties. You simply do not have the time for that. And your acquaintances and connections don't need that from you, either. You need to pick the people who mean the most to you and your experience, right now.

We all need weak ties, too—people who bring added perspective and diversify our networks. If you're on LinkedIn or any other social-media platform, you know how this works. It's the six degrees of separation concept. If you limit yourself just to the people whom you know well, then you're missing out on a world of opportunity based on the people they know well, and the people those people know well, and so on.

This is the value of the second- and third-level connections that are found on LinkedIn. You aren't directly connected to these people; you are connected to them *through* someone else. These people add value by broadening your network and your possible opportunities. But you're not going to go have brunch with those people. You're not going to reach out to them when you're in crisis or need a friend. That's what your strong ties are for. And you need to decide who those strong ties are, which ones are worthy of your time, and *which ones are making you worthy of theirs.* Do they align with the things you have decided are important to you?

Take a few moments to think about the people in your life. Start with your immediate, strongest ties—family and close friends. In what ways do they add to or detract from your ability to live your values? Then move to your next level—these might be people you would call friends or acquaintances. Then, next, think about weak-tie connections. And so on.

Take the time to reflect honestly and critically on the ways you are spending your time. Do the people you are spending time with feed you emotionally, intellectually, or otherwise? Or does that time drain you and leave you emotionally, intellectually, or otherwise exhausted?

You won't always have control over all of this—sometimes the people you work with will be the most draining on your emotional and intellectual resources, and you still have to spend a considerable amount of time with them—but are there steps you can take to increase the time with people who feed you, and decrease the time with people who drain you? And, are there certain values that remain empty? Are these gaps you need or want to fill?

Create three columns. First write in your five personal values in the left column. In the middle column, write down those people who you think support your ability to live that value. In the right column, write down those people who you think detract from your ability to live that value. You might also include a note about why that is.

Value	People (+)	People (-)

Once you have completed your lists, spend some time reflecting on what it means to you in the space below. **What have you learned about yourself**, your values, and your relationships now that you look at them this way?

You will have many people pass through your life, from work, from social events, from civic engagements, and from a multitude of places. When you can, take some time to think about the value people add to your life, how they align with the things you say you value, and how much you are willing to invest in that relationship.

This does not mean you have to be this cold, calculating person about acquiring and maintaining relationships, especially friendships. But as we've already discussed, you only have a limited amount of time. Are you willing to invest in someone as a deep relationship, or are they more of an acquaintance or a connection, or should they not be there at all? Just because someone *wants* to be part of your life does not mean you have to allow them to be there.

The organizational psychologist Adam Grant has developed a theory regarding relationship building and maintenance, which argues that we each are either a giver, a matcher, or a taker. According to his research, givers are those who willingly invest in others, regardless of what they may or may not get in return. Matchers try to balance giving and taking, and their willingness to give is predicated on an expectation of something in return. Takers try to get as much as they can out of others while contributing as little as possible.

Most of us fall in the matcher category. However, when it comes to metrics of success, it's the givers who stand out. Not only do givers tend to fall behind, constantly putting other people's needs in front of their own, givers also are the *most successful* people in organizations.[20]

What does this mean for you? As you work to build your networks and build community, you can't just expect other people to invest in you, without being willing to invest in them, in turn. Developing and maintaining relationships—real, quality relationships—takes work and takes effort. And doing that work—doing it from a place of genuine care for other people—does pay off.

Own Your Life Decisions

For many of you, your number-one category of strong ties will be your family, including parents and significant others. And, sometimes, this will be your number-one category of frustration, disappointment, and challenge as you move through these postcollege years. Adult relationships require resetting and reframing expectations and, like with all of the decisions you will be making, require being intentional about the type of life you would like to create, and with whom.

We all have to learn how to set boundaries, both personally and professionally, and that's true with regard to family, too. Sometimes the hardest steps to take are setting boundaries with family and redefining your relationship as one between adults. No matter the pressure you might feel, you need to remember that it's *your* life, and you're the only one who gets to live it. You get to choose who is there with you and how much influence they have over the choices and decisions you make.

Parents can be particularly challenging relationships to redefine. Just as you have perhaps always viewed your parents as role models, as wise counselors, as people who have "all of the knowledge," they have always seen and likely always will see you as their child who needs caretaking and the benefit of their guidance and wisdom and input into your decisions. Becoming an independent adult who no longer needs their permission to make decisions may always have been their goal, but that doesn't mean this transition is an easy one for them or for you.

Of course, you can always benefit from the wisdom of those more experienced than you are! But at some point in these first years into adulthood you will need to accept the reality that you no longer have to run decisions past your parents for their approval. You no longer need their permission to do things. Ask for their advice, yes. Their approval, no.

And, you no longer get to run to them to bail you out when you screw things up (which you will). Owning your life means *you* take responsibility, *you* give yourself approval and permission, and *you* accept full responsibility for the consequences of those decisions.

You may find this shift requires a pointed conversation to reset boundaries for your new adult relationship. Or, you may find this transition happens naturally over time, as they learn to let go and you learn not to ask quite so often. And at some point, hopefully far down the road, you will go through another transition, where you become the caretaker.

These are natural progressions of familial relationships. For now, take the time to notice what is happening and how you feel about it, and also notice how they are feeling about it. They spent a long time creating you and shaping you into the intentional, thoughtful, caring adult you have become. That's no small accomplishment. Thank them for doing that hard work.

Whether intentional or not, financial obligations often shape our relationships with our parents. If they just spent a lot of money on your college tuition, they may feel it has earned them the right to provide input into your life and career, or you may feel like you owe them that influence. If they are still covering your health insurance, car payments, or contributing to other bills, it may help you in the short term *and* it maintains those ties and makes it harder to cut the cord.

How do you start to redefine this relationship? Change the topic and the tone of those conversations. Just like with any mentor or wise counselor in your life, don't ask for permission on the actions you are taking, but share the steps you have taken and seek their feedback. Proactively share the steps you are taking to make adult decisions regarding your finances and your future so they can start to reenvision you as a competent, responsible adult. Like with any mentoring relationship, when they share feedback you don't like or agree with, or tell you what you are doing is wrong, thank them for their input and resist the temptation to argue with them or to defend your position. Ask questions and listen.

And, don't expect the change to happen overnight. You took twenty-two-plus years to get to this place. It's going to take some time to change that relationship.

Another change in postcollege relationships happens when your friends start to think about settling down, getting married, and talking about children. You may be considering these decisions for yourself, or you may be wondering how and when you are going to find "your person." Much like I am not going to be your financial adviser or your therapist, I am also not going to be your marriage and family counselor. But I am going to encourage you to continue to be reflective about your relationships, thoughtful about who you are letting into your life and why, and how those people impact the next steps you will take both personally and professionally.

Making the decision about a partner or a significant other as an adult is so much more than, *I think this will be a fun person to hang out with at this party.* Now you need to start to think about how this other person aligns with your values, and how he or she will or will not support the personal and professional decisions you will be making in the future.

Your decisions about the people you will let into your life, and why, and how you will spend your time, are and should be very personal ones. You get this one life, and you need to live it according to your values. This is not the time to compare yourself to other people, to wonder if you are "behind" in your life planning because other people are hitting certain milestone experiences, like marriage and children, before you are. Nor is it the time to race forward to hit those milestones because that is what you think you *should* do, or what other people are expecting of you. Rather, **you need to figure out what you want in your life**, and whether the person you have decided to spend time with wants the same things. Those are the only criteria that matter.

There is no magic process for attracting the "right" types of people into your life. Join organizations, do online dating, go to happy hours, join a church, and do what works for you to meet and get to know people. Whether friends, romantic partners, or professional acquaintances, as you gain more insight into who you are and what matters to you, make sure you are including more of the people who will help you to live out your values, and fewer of the people who prevent you from doing that.

If you want to get married and you are spending significant time with someone who does not, or you want to have children and he or she does not, then that is not a relationship that is going to end well for either of you. If you have significant differences of values and beliefs about the ways you want to live your lives, then that is going to produce considerable challenges in your future lives together, which warrants conversation.

Just like there is no magic process for finding a partner, and no crystal ball to look into for your career path, there is no secret code to determine if someone is *the someone* with whom you should spend the rest of your life. But here are a few questions you can ask yourself. Some of these may seem unromantic, but you have to be compatible in many senses to make a life with someone work.

- Do I genuinely like and care for this person?
- Do this person's goals and values align with mine?
- Can I see myself as part of this person's family, and him or her with mine?
- Do we have similar ideas about long-term planning, financial planning, and creating a future?
- Are the things I don't like about this person deal-breakers, or merely annoyances?
- How does this person behave in times of stress or a crisis?
- Does this person genuinely like and care for me?

Much more so than career decisions, long-term relationship decisions are both a leap of faith and can be difficult to change down the road. Don't ever make that decision before you are ready to do so. And, recognize that you will never have all of the information you need to make it.

At some point, you may start thinking about children. When is the best time for that to happen? I have heard, and you no doubt will, too, people say the best time to have children is early in your career before you have lots of obligations, and I have heard people say the best time to have children is after you are established in your career and are better able to call the shots. I have heard that the best time to have children is during graduate school, the best time to have children is pretenure, and the best time to have children is posttenure.

When is the best time? It's simply whatever you think is the best time for you.

That being said, you should know there is a limit on how long you will have to produce biological children, particularly if you are female. It can be easy to say, "I'll definitely do that someday," or, "I'm just focused on my career right now," or, "This just isn't the right time," and to put these decisions off for down the road.

The science is clear: it is statistically more difficult for a woman to get pregnant after the age of thirty-five, and those pregnancies come with a much greater risk of a range of birth defects.[21] Alternative methods (surrogates, IVF, etc.) and adoptions can cost many thousands of dollars and can take many years. These are not small considerations as you are looking toward the next five to ten years of your life.

It may seem strange to "plan" your personal life as you would your career, but these are important factors. Here are just some of the questions you (and your partner, if you have one) need to think about:

- Are you in a serious relationship now and have you talked about marriage and children? Is this someone you see yourself with, long term?
- By what age do you see yourself getting married, if you do?
- By what age do you see yourself having children, if you do?
- Do you plan to have biological children or to have children by other means?
- What is the financial burden you will assume if you have children?
- What is your organization's family leave policy?
- Will you come back to work or be a stay-at-home parent? How will that decision impact your career and your finances?
- If you are not in a relationship and plan to have children, when do you plan to do that? What steps will you take?

There are many other questions you can and should ask, of course. The point is that these are not decisions you should just leave up to chance. Owning your life is not just about owning your career development. Being an adult means you make the decisions, and you own the consequences. The time to start creating the life you want to live starts now.

Harness the Power of Groups

As an off-the-charts introvert, I tend to gravitate toward the one-on-one interaction and shy away from those occasions that put me into a room full of people, especially people I don't know. So-called "networking events" and places that require small talk are pretty much my nightmare. Sounds familiar? To some of you it most certainly will.

But we all have to master this skill to some extent, as there will always be those occasions that come up, both professionally and personally, which will require you to engage with people you don't know. The more you can become skilled at this practice, the more successful and less anxious you will be when thrown into these situations. And the good news is, you *can* practice it, and you *will* get better.

Whether introverted or extroverted, each one of us can benefit from finding our group. Seth Godin, in his work on tribes, notes, "One of the most powerful of our survival mechanisms is to be part of a tribe, to contribute to (and take from) a group of like-minded people." Tribes are about connection, and "connections lead to connections." Further, Godin goes on to articulate that tribes are a necessary ingredient for leadership. Forming or joining a tribe isn't hard, it turns out. All it requires is a shared interest and a means of communication.[22] You are likely part of one or more tribes right now and don't even realize it.

When I left Georgia a lovely group of women hosted a dinner for me, to send me off to new adventures in North Carolina. At the end of the evening, I found myself getting quite emotional as I looked around that table. Here were some of the most amazing colleagues and friends, mentors, role models, sponsors, and wise counselors, who had carried me and walked beside me on my journey, through graduate school, and challenges both professional and personal, for fifteen years.

My emotion came not from who they were; I had always known they were amazing. No, my emotion was due to my realization that I *had created this*, and that I was going to have to figure out how to do it again, in a whole new place. I recognized that there was no way I ever would have been half as successful as I had been in that place without that tribe. We all need a group, a support system of people who help us to understand and learn from our challenges and our successes.

Over the past few years, I have been working to recreate this experience through mentoring groups with young professionals. In various locations around the country, I bring groups of seven or eight young adults together over the course of eight to ten months to engage in facilitated conversation about how to navigate their personal and professional lives after college. We think and talk about many of the topics that are discussed in this book (indeed, those conversations have been the inspiration for this book):

- Who am I and what do I value?
- How do I align my personal and professional choices with my identity?
- How do I create positive life habits?
- How do I find friends and hobbies, which meaningfully contribute to my life?
- How do I intentionally reflect on my experiences?
- Where do I find mentors?
- How do I create a plan for what comes next?

Engaging in this activity as a group is another source of community-building and helps to normalize the experience. The transition from college to life after college, as you are now familiar, can be jarring and isolating. Just knowing that other people are going through the same things as you are can help affirm your experience. Indeed, it can be easy to fall into the trap postcollege of feeling like you have to project this image of having it all together, that you're living your best life, right now. Whereas the reality is, no one knows what they're doing, and everyone's struggling in some way. Creating a space that not only allows but asks for vulnerability is one way to counteract this temptation.

You don't need a "professional" to help you to create a group. You just need the energy to make it happen. It's like creating a book club, or any other small group experience, except that the content for the group is your life. Mentorship does not just have to come from above. Sometimes the most valuable voices we let into our lives are those of our peers.

Think about three or four people you know and think would benefit from a shared-mentoring group experience. Invite them in, and ask each of them to invite one other person in as well. Set some ground rules for open conversation, building trust, and maintaining confidentiality. Create expectations that everyone must own the process, and fully engage in the conversation. And see where the experience takes you.

I often see young people who complain about the lack of professional opportunity available to them and who wonder why no one is taking care of their personal and professional development. Don't be one of these people, waiting for someone to build your life and opportunities for you. And don't be like me, only able to recognize the powerful network I had built when it was time to leave it. **Own your growth and development.** Build the relationships you need, to gather wisdom and feedback into your experience. Pay attention to the people who are intentionally investing in you. There is great power to be found in the networks we build. Find your tribes and cultivate them.

Find Mentors, Sponsors, and Wise Counselors

While peer mentorship is a valuable thing to cultivate, you also need to find those more experienced mentors, sponsors, and wise counselors to help show you the way, to help inform your Knowing Why and Knowing How career competencies, to ask you those thought-provoking questions that lead to deep reflection, and to help you create and move forward on your goals.

As you may have already noticed, unless you are part of a formal mentoring program through your organization, these people don't just walk up and present themselves to you as they tended to do in college (though, I would argue it didn't exactly happen that way there, either). Indeed, **college is the last time you will have that many people who care that much about you, your choices, and your experience.** From now on, it's all on you to create those relationships for yourself. So, how do you go about doing that?

First, let's think about who these people are, and what the differences (and similarities) are between these roles. Over the past few years, you may have heard variations on, "You need to find a mentor," or "You need to find a coach," or "You need to find a sponsor," or "You really need an accountability partner." And what in the world is a "wise counselor"?

The truth is, we each need all of these people in our lives. And sometimes the same person will play multiple roles, and sometimes different people will play different roles. Sometimes a person may serve as a coach for a specific project and then change over to being a mentor. Indeed, outside of stated formal mentoring relationships, they may not even realize they are playing those roles when they are in them. Often we don't so overtly ask people to serve as mentors, or coaches, or sponsors to us. Instead, it's a process of intentional relationship building in which you, as the one seeking the support, work to identify and learn from the people whom you need.

And that means you need to be thoughtful and intentional about what you are looking for from other people. It all depends on your needs and what the other person is willing and able to give. This is why we all need diverse networks. It is no longer OK to expect one person to be the be-all, end-all, go-to person for all of your needs. It's an unreasonable expectation and very burdensome on the other person. It also doesn't allow for you to diversify your network and to bring different voices and perspectives into your journey.

So who are each of these people? Let's look at them each in turn, below.

> **Mentor**—someone with more experience than you in the area in which you are interested in being mentored; willing to engage in a personal and purposeful relationship over a period of time; provides feedback and wisdom based on his or her experience; facilitates your growth and development.

> **Coach**—someone who is skilled in asking questions, listening, and encouraging you to work toward your goals; not required to have experience in the area in which you are interested in being coached;

may provide feedback based on observed behavior or the coaching conversation; facilitates skill development, goal setting, and creating a plan of action.

Sponsor—someone who advocates for you; identifies opportunities and provides connections to those opportunities; promotes you to higher-ups for increased responsibility and advancement based on his or her personal, political, or organizational capital.

Accountability Partner—someone who will check in with you at agreed-upon points to ensure you are staying on course with your work toward your goals.

Wise Counselor—someone who periodically provides advice and wisdom, which may rise to the level of a "mentoring moment."

Networking Connection—someone who can suggest opportunities, provide introductions, and may pass along your résumé but may not rise to the level of a "sponsor."

There are certainly others you could add to this list. For me, there is a lot of overlap between these roles. For instance, I use coaching strategies in my mentoring conversations, and I believe being a sponsor, accountability partner, and wise counselor are all roles of great mentors. But I can also see where these might be distinct roles; that one might serve as a coach or accountability partner and not fully commit to a mentoring relationship.

It all depends on what you need and what the other person is willing and able to give. One key distinction between these roles is the level of relationship involved, from the deep relationship with a mentor down to no implied relationship with a networking connection.

In order to assess your network and the gaps you may need to fill, you should first return to the SMART goals you set in chapter 1. You might also want to look back at what you wrote down in chapter 2 and earlier in this chapter about how you want to better align your personal time with your values. After all, we need mentors and accountability partners for our personal lives just as much as our professional ones.

In the space provided on the following pages, first fill in your goals. Next, think about what you need to help you achieve those goals. Is it a mentor? A coach? A sponsor? Networking connections? You may find what you need is outside of these choices, for example, you may need to take a class or get a certification. Third, write in the names of the people you can think of who are currently in your network who could possibly fill those roles, or, if what you need is a resource and not a person, where you can find that resource.

Goal: *Ex: Identify three strategies to improve my work-life balance by the end of the year.*

Need: *Ex: Mentor, someone who seems to do this well*

Who/What: *Ex: Mary Ellen, Susan, Jack, Sylvia*

Goal:

Need:

Who/What:

Goal:

Need:

Who/What:

Goal:

Need:

Who/What:

You may find you have some blank spaces under the "Who/What" column and some gaps you need to fill. That's a great next step for follow-up.

Often someone will say something to me along the lines of, "I've never had a mentor," or, "I really want a mentor, how do I find one?" While I applaud the desire for personal and professional development, I also caution anyone who is starting from this place that you are not taking ownership for that development; rather, you are sitting back and complaining, "Why won't anyone mentor me?" From my experience, people who do the work get the mentorship they deserve. So before you go down that road, think about the following:

- **Am I paying attention?** Most likely there are people around you, right now, who are actively trying to advise and to guide you on your path. You simply aren't paying attention. So instead of asking the question, "Why won't anyone mentor me?" try asking the question, "Who is already mentoring me and how can I take more advantage of that relationship?"

- **Am I building intentional relationships?** Mentoring relationships are built upon two fundamental characteristics: they are goal oriented and they are relationship driven. Individually, you need to identify the goals you are prepared to work on. But you also need to work on building intentional relationships with other people before you ask them to support your goals.

- **Am I broadening my choices?** Don't limit potential mentors and connections to the people who are immediately around you. Diversify your network and the perspectives you are hearing. There can be a particular benefit to finding external mentors who can help you think through the political and cultural issues within your organization in a safe space. Think about people in professional organizations, civic organizations, social and alumni associations, and elsewhere. And seek out formal mentoring programs, which can expose you to people with whom you would not necessarily come in contact. Check to see if your organization offers a formal program you can join, and if not, think about whether you could start one. Chances are if you are looking for it, others are as well.

Once you have gotten honest about your needs, clarified your intentions, set some goals you are willing to work on, and looked at your network for someone with whom you feel comfortable, just **make the ask**. Share your goals and what you are asking for, both in terms of time and effort. Be reasonable: set a time frame of no more than six months, to start with. Be strategic and ask for what you need.

If you don't feel comfortable asking someone to be your mentor, just ask for their feedback or guidance, and work to build the relationship over time. There is a young woman whom I knew as a student who seeks me out every month or two for a catch-up conversation. We've never officially declared the relationship as mentorship, and I have no idea if she would define it as such. But she does the work to keep the relationship moving forward, and so I am honored to continue showing up in her life, in whatever way she needs.

Following are two examples of how you can **make the ask**. The first one is an example of someone looking for a wise counselor or networking contact. The second one is an example of someone looking for some coaching. Both, you will notice, are short and to the point: background, the reason for the contact, how they are connected, and the specific ask.

Dear Ms. Roberts,

I am a 2014 grad currently working for a trade association doing volunteer management and event planning. I am starting to explore options for my next step, and I am particularly interested in making a move to marketing and public relations on the agency side. I found your profile on LinkedIn, and see we have a mutual connection through Bob Smith. Would you have time for a brief conversation either over the phone or coffee to talk about your career path and to give me some feedback on navigating this transition? I am flexible to work with your schedule and I am attaching my résumé for more information.

Many thanks,

Sally West

Hi Bob,

I've recently been tasked with leading a project group to implement the new software integration. While I'm excited about the opportunity, this is the first time I have been put in a team-leadership role and I have a few concerns about keeping people motivated and on-task. I've noticed during the times we have worked together that you are quite skilled in both of those areas. Would you be willing to provide a bit of coaching to me as we get this project started? I'd love to have the opportunity to bounce some ideas off of you for your feedback. Happy to treat you to lunch or coffee for your time!

Many thanks,

Sally

Now, this is critical: if they say no, respect their answer, and say thank you and move on. **The absolute best mentor is the one who is willing to invest his or her time in you,** not one whom you have to beg. If they say yes, say thank you and get ready to do the work. And, as a note, anyone who is willing to invest in you truly is expecting nothing in return but your commitment, your respect for their time and their confidences, and your willingness to work on yourself. And every once in a while, a sincere note of gratitude is nice.

Get Engaged in Your Community

One of the best ways to *live where you live* and to build your network is to get engaged in your community. You probably heard many times over when you were in college how you were "part of a community" and what your responsibilities to that community looked like. That is even truer after college. You are now a tax-paying member of the place where you live, which means you need to educate yourself on the issues and the policies that are impacting that place and your fellow citizens who live there.

Indeed, while it is easy to become consumed by politics on the national stage, most of the policies that have direct impact on our lives are the local ones, ranging from education to roads to construction to trash collection. It may not seem very interesting or impactful now, but just wait until a local ordinance removes your recycling pickup and see how you feel about it then! It's not OK, as an adult, to say you don't know what's happening in the community where you live, or to claim ignorance about how you may or may not be contributing.

Beyond local politics, a great way to get involved is to find and to join local boards. Every community has certain high-focus issues, such as the arts or education, and organizations that take a leading role in serving philanthropic and civic needs. Each of these issues and organizations provides numerous opportunities to get involved in big and small ways. It's a great way to give back to the community with, as the saying goes, "your time, your talents, and your treasure."

And yes, your treasure—your financial commitment—is important and keeps these organizations running, but I would encourage you not to stop there. Find a way to volunteer. Join a committee. See if there is an "Under Forty" or "Young Professionals" board you can join. This gives you great community-leadership experience you can put on your résumé, and will expose you to a diverse group of leaders from across the community and help you build your network.

If you value faith and being part of a structured religious community, joining and becoming part of a church can provide access to another set of wise counselors and can provide opportunities to make an impact on social issues in addition to any personal meaning you may derive from the experience. Like any other organization, take the time to research the different churches in your area, meet the people, and learn about their values and beliefs and how they align with your own.

It can be easy to get overwhelmed by this process of building community or to feel obligated to join everything at once and to fill all available time. Just like when you were in college, you do no one any good by overcommitting and under-delivering. You will very soon develop a reputation as someone who cannot be counted on and cannot be trusted.

Instead, pick just one organization that holds personal meaning for you. Do your homework on its values, its mission, and the work it does. Find out how it uses its resources. If you are going to be an advocate for an organization, tie your reputation to the entity, and give up part of your precious resources to benefit it; you have to fully believe in what it does and how it does it.

It's up to you to create the community you need, to be successful in your life. Where you choose to live, and what you choose to do there, matters. But so do the relationships you create and cultivate, the life *you* build. Don't wait for someone to do it for you and then wonder why it didn't happen. It's all about making intentional choices. Choose to live where you live.

Practice Reflection

1. How are you living where you live? What strategies are you employing and what's working? Who do you know who is doing this well, and how?

2. How are relationships postcollege different from those you had in college?

3. What steps can you take to intentionally build both strong and weak ties?

4. How are you investing in your community?

5. How will you use this knowledge about yourself in the next year?

CHAPTER 4: PRACTICE REFLECTION

Gather Data…and It's All Data

Katie took a position straight out of college with a consulting firm based in Washington, DC. It had not been her plan to do so; she had been on a path toward a career in public relations, possibly in New York or California. But then her college boyfriend became her fiancé and he was determined to make it on the Hill, and Katie, of course, was going with him. On a whim she entered the consulting-firm recruiting process, and to her surprise found she not only loved it, she was good at it. Several years later, Katie is still with the same firm, and has received several promotions. She's leading project teams and managing people, though every once in a while some doubt creeps in about her abilities: "I've been supervising people for over a year now. I always looked at those people above me as having more knowledge or training than me. No one showed me how to do this." Some days she wonders if she should go back to school, or if she should explore opportunities elsewhere. "At what point are you too far down a path to make a change?" she wonders. She knows she's being set up for a great career at the firm. She's just not sure if it's the career she wants or if there's something better out there she might be missing.

Sound familiar? Whatever stage of our lives or careers we are in, each of us to a certain degree suffer through a bit of the FOMO mindset from time to time, otherwise known as "what if the grass is greener on the other side?" No matter how happy and fulfilled one may be in his or her job, it is tempting to consider what a different life might look like, and whether it might be better. It's easy to start wondering if one is truly happy, or just comfortable.

Many years ago a movie came out starring Gwyneth Paltrow called *Sliding Doors*. The premise to the movie was, through one small decision—

whether or not she gets on the Tube in London (this was during Gwyneth's British phase)—the entire trajectory of her life is altered. And over the course of the movie, we get to see both of those scenarios play out. We get to see her life if she does get on, and we get to see her life if she doesn't.

Of course, her character does not get to see those alternative realities; nor do any of us get to do so in our own lives. The truth is, your life is made up of a million decisions both large and small. As noted, every one of those decisions will have consequences, both positive and negative, and in some way will affect what comes after. But you rarely will have all of the information you need to make an absolutely certain decision. Our friend Katie, above, chose to accept her fiancé's proposal, chose to move to DC, and chose to go to work in consulting. Each of those decisions has led her to the moment she is in right now.

Rarely will you ever be able to say, with certainty, if I choose door number one my life will turn out this way, and if I choose door number two my life will turn out that way. Instead, at some point you have to gather all of the data you can to make an *informed* decision, and then you just have to take a leap and trust the net will appear.

So what then does this have to do with practicing reflection? Reflective practices—being mindful and present, seeking out feedback and data, identifying strengths and growth opportunities, and adopting a growth mind-set—are some of the best tools you have at your disposal to make these critical professional and life decisions. It's what will help you build your EQ—your emotional intelligence—which is what will help you be successful in work and life. It's what gives you the tools to navigate organizations and to overcome the impostor syndrome.

Building in reflective practices is one of the best habits you can adopt in these first years after college. And just like with building community, you already have many of the tools at your disposal. If there is anything our academic lives teach us to do, it's to gather and synthesize information, assess that information with a critical eye, and reflect on learning opportunities.

Now you just need to learn how to apply those strategies to your life.

Practice Mindfulness

"Mindfulness" might be one of the most overused words of the past few years, right up there with "self-care." I imagine you might have a more-than-visceral reaction to hearing both of those terms: rolling your eyes, smirking, and maybe a little fake gagging. If anything, these terms have become a rather convenient excuse for checking out and ignoring responsibilities. "Oh, I'm sorry. I can't come to that meeting because I'm choosing to be mindful and to practice self-care."

And sure, there may be value in setting boundaries and choosing to watch the latest episode of your favorite reality TV show over putting in yet another twelve-hour workday, but there is also value in knowing when to be present at work and in your life.

Mindfulness is about **being present**. It's about paying attention, whether it's paying attention to your breathing, or the path you're on, or the people and the places that surround you. Have you ever had the experience of arriving in a place and not remembering how you got there? Or reading something and having to go back and rereading it, because you can't remember what you read? It happens to all of us. We are all so busy, and so overscheduled, it becomes increasingly hard to pay attention to those things that are right in front of us, because we are so busy worrying about what's happening next.

Mindfulness is not just a fad or buzzword or new-age mantra. It's actually backed up by hard science into how our brains work. The science of neuroplasticity tells us the brain actually has an enormous ability to heal itself, and like any other muscle, can be taught to rewire itself through conscious thought and action.[23]

While there are, of course, enormous potential medical implications for this (recovery from injury, stroke, and other trauma), it also means we each have the ability to quiet the noise that is constantly being thrown at us from technology and a life that increasingly demands 24-7 engagement. While the "integrated lifestyle" may appeal to young professionals, it also has potentially devastating effects for mental functioning and ability to focus.[24] Practicing mindfulness is one strategy to rewire your brain for higher cognitive ability.

Being mindful is also about paying attention to what you are learning along the way. Philosopher and author, George Santayana, is famous for saying, "Those who cannot remember the past are condemned to repeat it." There is little use in having goals and plans for the future if you are not learning from your past and paying attention to your present. Making the decision to own your growth and development means being an active participant in your own life. It's OK to be forward-thinking, to have a plan and goals you are working toward. But don't get so consumed by what *may* happen and forget to participate in what *is* happening.

This is one of the gifts of effective mentorship. Mentors push us to think deeply about what is happening to us and why, and ask the **"What?"** **"So what?"** and **"Now what?"** questions that force us to make connections between what is happening and what we are learning from what is happening. Most of us in our day-to-day lives don't take the time to do this. We move from one to-do item on our task list to the next, from one meeting to the next, and ultimately, like Katie, from one career decision to the next, without stopping to think about why we are doing those things and what value they are bringing.

However, a moment or a day will come when we're forced to face the question: *How did I get here?* On the daily tasks and meetings and project lists, this moment may be surprising and require a bit of refocusing, but it probably won't be earth-shattering. But when it comes to your career and your life, you may not want to have a *Sliding Door* moment, ten years down a path that was decided by whether or not you got on a (metaphorical) train.

The good news is, while mentors can help, you can (and should) do this work for yourself and start to employ reflective practices both about your day-to-day tasks and larger career decisions.

Take a moment to reflect on and answer the following questions:

What? Describe a recent project or task you have been involved with. What happened? Were you successful? Did you accomplish your goals? What role did you play? What challenges did you encounter? *Be as objective as possible.*

So What? How do you feel about what happened? What did you learn about yourself as a result? *Be as subjective as possible.*

Now What? What will you do with what you learned, in the future? How will you use that knowledge to do things differently or the same? How will it impact how you approach future projects or tasks?

Now apply the same questions to your job role:

What? Describe your role or position. What are you expected to accomplish? Have you been successful? Have you accomplished your goals? What challenges have you encountered? *Be as objective as possible.*

So What? How do you feel about the work you have been doing? What are you learning about yourself as a result? *Be as subjective as possible.*

Now What? What will you do with what you learned, in the future? How will you use that knowledge to do things differently or the same? How will it impact future decisions or relationships?

This is not, and should not be, a one-time exercise. Add it into your to-do list, that every time you come to the end of something—a project or a task—or every time you move through an experience like a major life or career decision, you will take the time to do a postmortem on it, and ask the What, So What, and Now What questions. **Don't miss the learning moments.** Don't be so focused on getting to the next thing that you miss the opportunity to reflect on and learn from the thing that is right in front of you. And if you can discuss these learning moments with a mentor, all the better.

Gather Data...and It's All Data

Frequently, I have a conversation with a young professional (I'll call her Meg, for the sake of this example) that goes something like this:

> *Me: I understand you're facing a career decision. Walk me through your decision-making process.*
>
> *Meg: Well, on the one hand I have this good job, and I really like my coworkers, but I feel like I'm coming to the end of my opportunity to be*

challenged. Like, I've done it all, now. And I don't see a path forward, necessarily. And on the other hand, I may have the chance to do something else at another company. A friend who works there reached out to me and said the company may be posting something soon and wants to know if I want to submit my résumé. She seems pretty happy there.

Me: So what are you going to do?

Meg: I don't know. I don't want to just jump ship at the first opportunity that comes along, but at the same time I do want to grow and develop in my career. But I don't know if I'll get that at this other place, either. What if I go there and it's worse? But what if I stay and I miss out on a great next step? How do I figure out what the right decision is? What do you think I should do?

This is just another version of the *Sliding Doors* dilemma. Do you get on the train or not? And like Gwyneth Paltrow's character, you will never have all of the information you need to make the "right decision," which rarely ever exists.

But you can gather more information to make a *more informed* decision. And this doesn't just apply to moments of decision (or indecision, as it were). Everything—every experience, every interaction, every relationship—is data, and a learning opportunity for you. **How are you collecting the data you need** to create intentional experiences, relationships, and personal and professional opportunities that better align with your goals and values?

Building in those mindful, reflective practices about your own actions and experiences is one place to start. Think critically about what is happening to you, and what you are making happen, and what you are learning from it. Ask the What?, So What?, Now What? questions. But you also should apply a critical eye to the behaviors and actions of others as well as to your environment, and apply the same reflective mind-set to those as well.

Here are some questions to get you started:

What do you like and not like about your supervisor's management style?

What do you like and not like about your current work environment?

What does success look like in your organization? What gets rewarded? What happens when someone makes a mistake or does not meet his or her goals?

What do career paths look like there? How is career development rewarded?

Based on your answers to these questions, what questions about your career or working life do you want to answer next?

There are many other questions you could add to this list, of course, some of which have been mentioned in previous chapters. One set of questions I particularly like is from Marcus Buckingham and Curt Coffman and their work for Gallup on strengths-based leadership. There they identify the twelve questions that form the basis for great management.[25] Included are questions like these: *Do I know what is expected of me at work? In the last seven days, have I received recognition or praise for doing good work? Does the mission/purpose of my company make me feel my job is important?* These twelve questions are a great reflective exercise for you to work through periodically.

There are no right or wrong answers. What matters is that you are thinking through the questions and critically assessing what your answers mean *for you.*

Don't just let life happen to you, throwing up your hands and saying, "No one ever gave me an opportunity! It's not my fault my life turned out this way!" The world is *not* your oyster, despite what you might have been told, and not everything is within your control. You *will* work for terrible bosses who keep you from advancing, you *will* have coworkers who aren't supportive team players, and you *will* watch people get promoted over you who don't deserve it.

You cannot control the behaviors of other people. You can control your reaction to these experiences. Do they keep you down, or do you learn from them? Similarly, with the positive experiences, how do you react when someone reaches out to you and supports your growth, and when people make room for you in their lives? Pay attention to what's happening and why. **It's all data,** which should inform your next steps.

And you don't have to go it alone. If you aren't sure about the answers to some of these questions, find a mentor you can talk to, or do some informational interviews with more experienced coworkers to see how they would answer. Figure out which bits of information you are missing.

In the case of our previous example, Meg was trying to make a career decision without knowing anything about a possible opportunity, which has not been posted yet. She's already at salary-negotiation point, and she has not even applied. And, she's completely discounting any possible opportunity at her current company, without asking the questions to get the answers she needs. Maybe her boss isn't aware she is interested in growth opportunities. Maybe there is a plan in place for a promotion in six months, but it just hasn't been communicated yet. You have to gather the data. **You have to ask for what you need.**

There's a line from that old movie, *Jerry Maguire*: "Help me, help you." Well, you need to help other people to help you. Don't expect them to know what you want or what you need.

As part of your data-gathering process, you need to be able to identify objectively your own strengths and opportunities for growth. More than likely, wherever you are, you will have some sort of an annual performance review that will give you some of this feedback. If you're lucky, this process will happen more than once a year, but most organizations and managers don't and won't. And that's because most organizations and managers don't do performance reviews well, which in turn makes them a burdensome (and less-than-useful) process. By the end, everyone is exhausted, hardly anyone is better for it, and everyone is pretty OK with waiting another year before doing it again.

The way a performance review *should* work is that it should be a culmination of a year's worth of ongoing conversations about what you're doing well and your areas for improvement. It should be an opportunity to reflect on your growth and development, to acknowledge challenges and celebrate successes. And, it should be tied into clear, measureable goals you have set for yourself (or have been set for you). In other words, there should be no surprises when you get to annual review time.

Unfortunately, in organizations where these sorts of ongoing developmental conversations aren't happening, the annual review process can be the source of considerable angst. It's usually tied to the annual compensation-review process, which ups the pressure. And, once the process is over, a copy of your review will be placed in a file somewhere with human resources, where it will stay, forever.

But even if your organization or manager does not do this process well, it doesn't mean it has to be anxiety-ridden for you. Think about how you can take ownership for your own growth and development. If no one is asking you to set quarterly or annual goals, there is nothing stopping you from doing that on your own. Once a quarter, set three to four SMART goals connected to your work with associated action steps for achieving them. Share these goals with your supervisor and ask for feedback.

Not only does this demonstrate to your supervisor that you care about your work and your development; it demonstrates initiative and engages him or her in the conversation around your future. You're not just sitting back, waiting for someone to tell you what to do and to give you opportunities. You're owning your career development and engaging your supervisor in the process.

In addition to seeking feedback on your goals and asking the What? So What? and Now What? questions for yourself, you should get into a regular practice of asking for feedback on your work from your supervisor, peers, and other work colleagues. Not only does this demonstrate your interest in working on yourself; the more often you ask for feedback, the less painful that conversation becomes. This is how you develop your self-awareness of your strengths and growth opportunities.

The difficulty with asking for feedback is that very few people have been trained in delivering feedback well, so it often ends up being ineffectual or hurtful. And, someone who is constantly demanding, "Tell me how I can seek out additional opportunities here," quickly becomes an annoyance. You need to learn to balance gathering productive feedback with not asking others to do your work for you.

The best feedback is **immediate, objective,** and **impactful.** *Immediate* means not waiting too long to deliver feedback to another person (thus the problem with the aforementioned annual reviews). *Objective* means the feedback should be based on concrete, observed behaviors or actions, as opposed to personality differences or hearsay. And *impactful* means the feedback clearly demonstrates how those observed behaviors or actions impacted others, either positively or negatively.

Think back to the last time someone gave you a bit of feedback. Was it immediate? Was it objective? Was it impactful? Most likely it was missing one or more of these elements. You may have walked away from the conversation wondering what you were supposed to do next, or feeling like a relationship had been damaged. Neither of those outcomes is very helpful.

An example of a well-delivered feedback statement is: "Yesterday in our team meeting (*immediate*), when you were on your phone (*objective, observed behavior*), it conveyed the impression you were not interested in your colleagues and their work (*impact on others*). Or: "Yesterday in our team meeting (*immediate*), when you volunteered to lead our design committee (*objective, observed behavior*), it really demonstrated a commitment to our core values of collaboration and teamwork (*impact*)."

As someone who is seeking feedback, you can help other people by asking two simple questions:

1. On (X project) what are the two to three things you think I did particularly well?
2. What are the one to two things you think I could have done differently or better?

There are several keys to asking for this sort of feedback. First, you want to hang it on a specific work project. This gives the other person a tangible subject to craft the feedback around (as opposed to the more general, *what do you think I do well?*). You are giving him or her the concrete, observed behaviors or actions on which you would like the feedback.

Second, you want to ask for the feedback close to the conclusion of the project, making it immediate, but give the person a little time to reflect on it. So, ask for a meeting in a week's time to discuss the answers to these two questions. Don't hit him or her with it cold, or you're likely not going to receive feedback that will be meaningful to you.

Third, and most importantly, when you have the feedback conversation, refrain from defending yourself when you hear something you don't like. You can ask questions for clarification or to gather additional information, but that's it. At the end of the conversation, say thank you and tell the other person you will be reflecting on his or her feedback.

And then, be sure you do just that! Not every bit of feedback has to be acted upon, but **it's all data** for you to consider. If you are consistently hearing things like, "You did a great job getting this project done, and you exceeded all of our task expectations, but in the future you should think about how you can engage your coworkers more in the planning process," it's easy to focus on the "exceeding expectations" part and to ignore the fact that your coworkers don't think you're much of a team player. And that's going to impact whether or not you will be considered for promotions or additional responsibilities in the future. It's your choice whether you want to work on your team-building skills or not. Just remember: all choices have consequences.

Create Habits of Lifelong Learning

The process of seeking feedback, identifying strengths and growth opportunities, and reflecting on behaviors and experiences are ways we start to create habits of lifelong learning. Indeed, by working through the process of identifying and developing your career competencies (chapter 1), you're already well on your way to adopting what Carol Dweck has now-famously coined as a "growth mind-set," or the belief that our abilities aren't fixed and dependent solely upon innate talent.[26]

People who adopt a growth mind-set aren't unrealistic or believe they can do anything. We each have individual natural gifts and talents. But we each also have the opportunity to grow and to build our strengths in multiple areas. I am not a naturally gifted or talented musician. But that doesn't mean I can't learn to play an instrument, with dedication and practice.

The same principle applies to our personal and professional lives. We each have the ability to adopt behaviors of continual learning, to stay naturally curious, and to seek out knowledge about ourselves, our careers, our organizations, and our industries. In fact, this is one of the key ways you can differentiate yourself from your coworkers and peers.

Be the person who has done his or her homework, who has studied trends and benchmarked peers and competitors for best practices and anticipated challenges. Figure out what the trade publications are in your industry, and make a practice of reading them. Find a local and a national newspaper to scan to stay up-to-date on current events. Each of these activities builds your abilities to be a strategic thinker, to problem-solve and contribute to high level conversations with knowledge and authority, and to be an educated member of society.

Unless you are in graduate school, creating intentional paths and processes for learning after college is something *you* must do for yourself. And, much like all of the other things you are working to "fit in," in your limited available time, you will need to figure out how and when to make these opportunities happen.

If you're lucky, your workplace may provide regular professional-development opportunities in the form of classes, workshops, webinars, and mentoring programs. As much as possible (or required), take advantage of these subsidized learning moments. But be strategic about it: you don't want to become the person in the office who is constantly absent and not doing your work because you are attending some class.

This is a great moment to revisit the "Knowing How" career competency. What are your knowledge and skill gaps for success in your current role? Now comes the hard work of figuring out how to fill those gaps. And remember, learning postcollege comes in all sorts of forms, through books and articles, through online courses, through in-person workshops and certifications, through formal graduate-degree programs, and through mentoring and coaching relationships. The good news is that in this highly connected knowledge-based economy, there is no shortage of information available for you to acquire. It's up to you to figure out which information is relevant, and how to acquire it.

Creating habits of lifelong learning is one way to build your emotional intelligence, or EQ. Research has argued that EQ accounts for up to 58 percent of job performance and is the "strongest driver of leadership and personal excellence." Further, "every point increase in EQ adds $1,300 to an annual salary."[27] Sounds important, doesn't it? So what is it and how do you do it?

In short, EQ is "your ability to recognize and understand emotions in yourself and others and your ability to use this awareness to manage your behavior and relationships."[28] More specifically, EQ has four components:

- **Self-awareness:** your ability to recognize your emotions and mood and how it impacts others.
- **Self-management:** your ability to manage your impulses and moods, and to think before acting or reacting.
- **Social awareness:** your ability to gauge accurately the emotions of others through listening and observing.
- **Relationship management:** your ability to build rapport, build networks, and to inspire trust.

People with low EQ lack the ability to receive and respond to critical feedback in an appropriate manner, get defensive when their ideas are challenged, and lack the ability to moderate their temper. People with low EQ lack the ability to see themselves the way others do and may publicly declare themselves to be a great coach, mentor, connector, and leadership role model while their colleagues and employees shake their heads and roll their eyes. People with low EQ often suck the available air out of the room and lack the ability to develop and maintain effective interpersonal relationships. For these and many other reasons, it should be obvious why EQ is valuable, both personally and professionally.

Fortunately, unlike IQ, your emotional intelligence can be developed. Here are a few tips for you to try to get started:

- **Pay attention to your emotional, verbal, and physical responses.** Write down your responses to different work and life experiences. What patterns do you start to notice over time?

- **Practice not responding.** The next time you have the urge to jump in and argue a point, try taking a step back. What were you going to say and why? How does it feel to sit one out? What was the result of you not making yourself heard?

- **Seek out feedback.** Ask a trusted friend or colleague to observe you in different situations and to give you feedback on how you engage with others and how you manage your own responses. Try to resist the urge to defend yourself, but simply listen and ask questions for clarification, and then reflect on what you heard.

We all have areas we need to develop. But you don't have to learn everything at once. Life is a journey of becoming. As Kouzes and Posner note in their book, *Learning Leadership*, "Growth is always at the edges, just outside the boundaries of where you are right now."[29] Start by building small habits of lifelong learning, which allow you to critically assess where you are and take strategic steps to where you want to be.

Be an Organizational Learner

Sometimes the most challenging aspect of learning how to be successful at work is figuring out how to navigate the organization itself. How do you get through and around the people who may be holding you back or putting up roadblocks? How do you learn to do things in the right ways, which are rewarded by the institutional culture and structure? When is the right time to speak up and when do you need to shut up, and when can you negotiate for a promotion or a raise? How do you get over the impostor syndrome and finally feel like you deserve to be there?

It's a lot to figure out, and you don't have a lot of time to learn it. As our friend Katie notes in the beginning of this chapter, the likely scenario is that no one is going to show you how to be successful in your current role or your future ones. Very few organizations build in developmental on-boarding programs that tell you exactly what you need to know to do your job and to create successful relationships with your coworkers and superiors. They expect you to come in knowing how to do that work!

So, how do you get up to speed? A great starting place is to be someone who is deeply reflective, who sets goals, and takes a strategic view toward his or her career, and who builds relationships with mentors and wise counselors who can help inform and guide the way.

Start with some simple questions:

1. What is expected of me in this role?

2. What does success look like as defined by my supervisor and my coworkers?

3. Who are the key influencers here? Whose voice gets privileged and whose gets silenced?

4. What steps can I take to distinguish myself from my peers?

5. Whom do I need to build intentional relationships with in order to achieve my goals and to be successful?

If you cannot answer these questions for yourself, then you need to seek out guidance from others. Don't make assumptions about how others view you, your role, and your value to the organization. Seek out feedback and then use those reflective skills you have developed to incorporate that feedback into your practices and your work.

No matter how intentional, thoughtful, and relationship-oriented you are, there is a level of organizational politics you will never be able to overcome. Certain people just make it their life's mission to sabotage others out of fear, jealousy, low self-esteem, or a host of other issues. Particularly when you are at the lowest rungs of the organizational hierarchy, your social and political capital is going to be so low you aren't going to have a lot of room to navigate around these issues. So then you are confronted with a choice: you can spend your time being irritated and angry about it, you can spend your time doing great work and controlling the things you can control, or you can spend your time looking for another job.

Clearly, of these choices, I would encourage you to focus on option number two, and use option number three only if the situation gets so toxic you feel you truly have no other choice. But it's always worthwhile to think about what the other person needs or wants from you. For instance, you may feel you are being micromanaged by your supervisor, as though he or she doesn't trust you to get your work done on time or to produce a successful product, because he or she is constantly hounding you for check-in reports on your progress. Your first reaction may be to feel frustrated and demoralized because you feel like you're being treated like a child.

But before you go there, it's worth taking a step back to consider *why* your supervisor feels this way. Perhaps *he or she is* being micromanaged by *his or her* supervisor, which has led to him or her feeling under pressure to be able to report on your progress at any moment. Perhaps he or she has had a bad experience in the past with prior employees who have overpromised and under-delivered, leaving your supervisor holding the bag and looking foolish. Perhaps, honestly and truly, he or she just doesn't trust you.

Whatever the reason is, your goal should be to create trust and to figure out how you can make your supervisor look good to his or hers. Instead of waiting for him or her to come to you demanding an update, create a regular check-in process to anticipate those needs. Be intentional in how you communicate your progress and seek out feedback to make sure you are doing things in the right ways. Ask *how* he or she would like this information communicated, whether it's in person, via e-mail, or otherwise. Don't assume your preferred method of communication is his or hers. Act on feedback and circle back to let him or her know you have done so. Ask your supervisor what you can do to contribute to his or her success, and then do those things.

You may not fix his or her micromanaging ways, but you will build trust and demonstrate you add value over time. And that's what "playing politics" looks like. You still always want to do great work and be able to look at yourself in the mirror at the end of the day and feel like you worked as hard as you possibly could. Great relationships without the work to back it up is just schmoozing and is noticed by others more than you might think. But navigating organizational politics is almost always about navigating relationships. Having great mentors who can guide you and advocate for you is invaluable to learning this skill, as is developing your EQ.

Part of organizational learning is also figuring out when is the right time to ask for a promotion or a raise. There are no hard and fast rules to this, and a lot depends upon the culture of your organization. **You have to learn to "read" the culture.** Do people earn promotions at set points, like every two years? Are promotions solely based on merit, and does hard work get rewarded? Or is it about who you know more than the work you do?

These and many other factors will influence whether it is the right time for you to have this conversation with your supervisor. You need to be able to read the organization and your superiors, and anticipate how they may react. And if you don't know how to do this, reach out to a trusted adviser or mentor first.

Bearing in mind all of that, here are some good rules to stick by:

1. **Has your work changed in some significant way?** Are you now doing higher-level work than you previously were, which warrants a higher title? Generally speaking, promotions and raises (other than general, annual cost-of-living raises, which have nothing to do with the work you are doing) don't come along for doing the same work you've always done. You need to be able to demonstrate increased responsibilities, abilities, and outcomes.

2. **What is your market value?** Do your homework. Go to Glassdoor.com or other sites to compare your salary with those of others at your same level. How do you compare? Be prepared to make a case for yourself.

3. **Find sponsors.** It's great for you to be able to make a case for yourself, and that is a skill you should practice. But it's a stronger argument if others at higher levels than you are advocating on your behalf. Work to develop relationships with people who can see your value and are willing to go to bat for you.

4. **Seek out additional opportunity.** Sometimes you have to make the case for the role you want, before you get there. Demonstrate interest in higher-level roles by seeking out people and project-management roles that both build your skills and add real demonstrated value to the organization.

5. **Be prepared to negotiate.** Before you walk into the room, you need to be clear on what you want, and what you're willing to walk away both from and with. Where are you going to draw the line in the sand? Are you willing to walk away from the job, if needed? If the organization is not able to give you a raise at this point, can you negotiate for something else, like additional professional development?

6. **Use the performance review as a time to review your position description.** Before the review, take the time to look over the description and make changes to your work duties as appropriate (these should reflect what you're actually doing, not aspirations). Send this in advance to your supervisor and ask to make it part of the review conversation. This is a nice way to segue into the potential-promotion conversation.

7. **Own your career path.** *Do say:* I'm looking for additional opportunities to develop my people and project-management skills, as I'm very interested in advancement here and would like to have that conversation. *Don't say:* I see you gave me a "meets" instead of an "exceeds" expectations on my performance review in a few areas. What exactly do I have to do to get an "exceeds"? The first invites a conversation and demonstrates personal responsibility. The second is defensive and demonstrates an unwillingness to work. (Here's a hint: If I have to tell you what it takes to get an "exceeds," then you're not getting one.)

The raise and promotion conversation is never an easy one, though if you are working in a place that actively supports your growth and development, it should be. If you've done the work of developing your career competencies and reflecting on your strengths and opportunities for growth, and built your self-awareness to allow you to honestly and objectively own your worth, it should not be hard to speak up for that.

But often our psyches get in our way, and we talk ourselves out of these conversations, believing we're not worth it, or we don't deserve more than what we have. This is **what's known as the impostor syndrome**, and we all suffer from it at one point or another. As one young professional put it recently, "How do I balance getting over the impostor syndrome and owning my skills and strengths, and not coming off as an entitled millennial who feels like I'm owed something?" Or, according to another, "There's this weird balance of learning how to be grateful for the opportunities I've been given, and recognizing what I've earned."

Sounds familiar? You experience the impostor syndrome when you're constantly looking over your shoulder, wondering when you will be "found out" as someone who should not have been let in. You experience the impostor syndrome when you look at a job posting and you don't apply for it because you can't say you have achieved every single bullet they are looking for. You experience the impostor syndrome when you get promoted and then wonder, "Who let me lead all of these people? I have no idea what I'm doing!" Well you know what? Neither do the rest of us; welcome to the club. It's time to put on your big boy or girl pants and get over it.

There *is* a balance between owning your skills, abilities, and smarts, and being a complete narcissist who thinks he or she can do no wrong. Having humility is a good thing. Recognizing you're not great at everything is a good thing. Knowing when you need help, and asking for it, is a good thing. And that's why your EQ matters so much. People with strong EQ aren't narcissists.

So how do you get over the impostor syndrome? One of the best ways is to find a mentor, someone who will objectively point out your strengths and growth areas and can give you some affirmation when you are doubting yourself. Find someone who will look at that job description and tell you why you should (or shouldn't) apply for it. Seek out people who have been in your role, whom you look to as role models, and ask them how they got over *their* impostor syndromes. We all have it, at some point or another. Connecting to others and learning from their experience is one of the best ways to normalize behavior.

Finally, this is a good time to recognize and remember some fundamental truths about work:

- **No one gives you a job out of pity.** You are there because you earned it and someone thought that based on your experience and credentials you deserve to be there. What you do after that is up to you.

- **Just because you're working for and with grown-ups does not mean they will behave like grown-ups.** This one can be jarring when you first enter the professional world. Just because someone has the title of "manager" or is in a position of leadership, it doesn't mean he or she has the first clue about performing that role. Don't spend time trying to fix him or her, but do learn from him or her. Mentorship comes in all sorts of forms.

- **Age is just a number.** At some point you will move into a managerial role, and possibly be managing people who are older than you are. No longer does work operate on such strict hierarchies. Always be respectful to everyone. As the old saying goes, the people you see on your way up will be the same people you see on your way back down.

- **No one will ever care as much about your growth and development as you.** Don't wait for someone else to do it for you, to give you opportunities, and to open doors. Make it happen for yourself. Take ownership for your career and your life.

Remember Gwyneth Paltrow and her character in the movie *Sliding Doors*? Here's the funny thing about that (and let it be said, spoiler alert for those who want to see it): at the end of the movie, both characters end up in very similar places.

So maybe, all the planning, and angst, and worrying about where we're going to be in twenty years is a bit overblown. Maybe, instead of worrying about where we will be, we should be more focused on where we are.

Be present in your life. Take ownership for it. Learn from the journey.

Practice Reflection

1. What are the one to two specific reflective practices you will build into your work and life?

2. What do you learn about yourself from the What, So What, and Now What questions?

3. What do you need to work on to build your EQ?

4. What has been your experience with the impostor syndrome?

5. How will you use this knowledge about yourself in the next year?

CHAPTER 5: OWN WHAT'S NEXT

"How do you know when it's time to make a change?"
— Andrew, Young Professional

Andrew moved to San Francisco after graduation, seeking a bit of adventure. He had a couple of friends who were moving there too, and they found a small apartment they could share and jobs to pay the bills. None of them were doing what they would call "passion" work, but they were having fun and didn't really care. But after a few years one of Andrew's roommates was in a serious relationship that was headed toward marriage and the other was applying to graduate school. Andrew had been promoted and he could see staying there long term, but he wasn't certain it was what he wanted. In truth, he had no idea what he wanted. "I like my job right now, and I like my life. But all of my friends are starting to get married, are settling down, and talking about having kids. Is that what I'm supposed to be doing? Am I supposed to go to graduate school? Am I supposed to stay here? How do you know when it's time to make a change? How do you know this isn't where you're supposed to be?"

There are going to come points, during this lifelong career and life journey, when you are going to start to feel an itch to make a change. Maybe work isn't going quite as well as you had hoped, and you're starting to realize that what you thought you wanted to do when you graduated from college isn't what you want to do at all. Maybe you moved to a place you no longer care for, or you're just ready for a new adventure. Maybe you're in a committed relationship that is leading to that next step, and you're having conversations about home ownership and children and other serious life decisions. Maybe, despite the fact that when you left college you swore you would never go to school again, you're ready to think about graduate school.

Maybe you're just ready for something different.

The title of this book is *Five For Your First Five*, and this fifth chapter is all about owning what's next, because life doesn't end at year five. Nor will you have everything figured out by then. But hopefully at this point in the book you're a little bit wiser, a little bit clearer on who you are and where you are headed, and a little bit less stressed about the uncertainty of it all. And it doesn't necessarily get less uncertain, as you go. But armed with more information and *more data*, you are better equipped to step into that uncertainty and make some smart, informed choices about work, life, and the people who are sharing this journey with you.

By the end of this chapter, you will create a plan, which may include a new job, a new location, new relationships, or graduate school. Like our friend, Andrew, you too may be struggling with these questions: "How do you know when it's time to make a change? How do you know *this* isn't where you're supposed to be?" The short answer is, you don't, and you won't, not with complete certainty. But the longer answer is, armed with enough data, you will be better equipped to make a more informed and smarter decision. Let's figure out how.

Make Informed Decisions

The beginning of your professional life is all about learning how to be a professional and learning how to do work. Over the first few years of work you gain invaluable insight about how to show up to work every day, how to work with and for other people, how to translate a college work ethic into one that works in the professional world, how to navigate organizational politics, how to seek out professional mentors and sponsors, and a whole host of other things we have discussed in the previous four chapters.

During your first few years out of college, you may discover a passion or an interest or a skill you weren't aware of before. You may find the thing you thought was going to be so amazing when you were in college turns out to be not so amazing when it becomes your daily focus. You may discover some truths about yourself in terms of the type of work you want to do and the type of life you want to live, and the trade-offs you are willing to make to make those things happen.

Just as your first year of college is all about learning how to be a college student, the first few years of work are all about learning how to be a working adult. Once you acquire some tangible experience to put on your résumé and know a little more about yourself, your strengths, and your goals, it's time to think about what may come next. It's time to create a plan.

But not just any plan. You don't want to get so narrowly focused you're not available or open to opportunities that may present themselves to you along the way. You still don't need a twenty-year plan. If you want to set a twenty-year vision for your life—*In twenty years I will be the top neurosurgeon in the country*—that's perfectly fine. But as far as a plan goes, keep it to five years or less.

Even if you're working toward a long-term future vision, you still need to be able to be present in your life. And, as you've likely already discovered, there are a lot of things that can happen in five years that make you want to or need to change your long-range plan.

As you are aware, there are some who claim that individuals in your generation will have upward of twenty different jobs over the course of their lifetimes, while others note that the career paths of millennials are not that different from the generation that preceded them.[30] What does this conflicting research mean for you? Nothing more than that you should recognize you do not have to create a career path based upon defined upward trajectories at one organization.

Instead, more and more of today's employees are crafting their careers with an entrepreneurial mind-set across a multitude of organizations, content to move on when they are no longer getting what they need in terms of personal and professional opportunities and growth. A recent article in *Fast Company* dubbed this "The Four-Year Career," describing both the average time professionals are staying in one role and the process of moving from role to role to craft one's own career path.[31] An entrepreneurial mind-set is no longer an option; it's a core career competency that belongs in your Knowing How list, in any industry.

This movement is not unique to millennials, although it has certainly become more pervasive among them. Anecdotally, I know many young adults who would love to find an organization they could see themselves sticking with over the course of a lifetime. They crave that sense of stability and finding a place where the mission aligns with their values, and where the leadership provides ongoing growth and development opportunities through stretch assignments, mentoring, creating intentional career paths, and support of an integrated work and life. Create an organization that does those things, and you will have potential employees beating down your doors.

But these are things almost all employees want. We all want to learn and to grow through our work. We all want supportive mentoring and coaching. We all want work that gives us meaning, in whatever ways we define that. We all want a work life that understands we also need an actual life, and supports the alignment or the integration of those two things to our individual benefit. That isn't being "stereotypical millennial." That's being human.

Nearly twenty years ago, I had a colleague tell me, "You should change jobs every three to five years." Over the course of my career, I have discovered that for many people, there is a lot of truth in that statement. It is not a universal truth, of course; very few such maxims exist. But looking back over my own career, I see that every three to five years or so is when a pretty big job shift happened and sometimes even more frequently.

When I reflect upon those moments, here is what I discover: that three-to-five-year window is roughly the point at which you should have mastered something and are likely to want a new challenge or growth opportunity, which means it is time to go do something else; or, it is the point at which you realize you are never going to master it, which means it is time to go do something else. There is some truth for each of us in "The Four-Year Career."

But what does "something else" look like? The hard part is there is no one answer to this, or at least not one I can give you. This is the part you have to figure out for yourself. Sometimes it's an obvious choice between two distinct alternatives, one that is safe and known and an easy win, and the other that is challenging and uncertain and a potential for failure. Sometimes it's finding a new challenge right where you are.

That's what happened with me. Although I have held a multitude of roles over the course of my career, changing official titles at least every three to five years if not more frequently, I have worked for precisely two organizations postcollege. Sometimes a change looks like moving departments, or changing to a new team, or adding a new set of responsibilities within the same organization. And sometimes it means a move to a new organization, a new location, or gaining additional credentials through graduate school (which may also mean a new location).

So we find ourselves with the following questions:

- When do I know it's time to make a change?
- How do I figure out what the change should be?
- How do I get there from here?

Let's look at each of them in turn.

Know When It's Time to Make a Change

There is a tricky balance between knowing it's time to seek out additional opportunity and challenge and perhaps being too quick to dismiss early professional opportunities as not being "enough," in whatever way you define that: not challenging enough, not big enough, or not worthy enough for someone with your experience and education. And, certainly, those things may be true. Are you underemployed? Are you working at a job that someone without equivalent skills, experience, or credentials could also do? Are you spending a good part of your day surfing the Internet to fill the time?

Sometimes there is value in those roles; for example, if it allows you to live in a part of the world you would not otherwise go to, or if it's helping you pay off loans and other bills, or if you are gaining critical skills and experiences and access to a network you would not otherwise have the opportunity to gain.

But if that job is simply the working equivalent of living on your parents' couch—in other words, if you're just killing time and if you are not learning or building your skill set—then that's probably worth examining. Every experience leads to the next one. Being underemployed now, without a good reason you can explain to a future employer, will only make it that much harder to get the more challenging opportunities down the road.

More often, what I see are not young people who are underemployed but young people who feel undervalued and who actually are in great entry-level positions but who quickly become bored or disillusioned with that experience and are too eager to make a change. Believing they are expected to have twenty-plus jobs in their lifetimes, they hit the two-year mark (or sooner) and think, *Well, I've done my two years; it's time to make a change.*

First of all, let's remember **it's OK to be happy**. The twenty-jobs thing is not a prescription. It's an observation of what people think is happening. If you like your job, like the people you're working with, feel you are getting great professional opportunities and building a life that holds meaning for you, great! You win. The grass is not, in fact, always greener on the other side.

And second, after a college experience that surrounded you with support systems and mentors and people who genuinely cared about your progress, you may have entered your first professional experience and discovered you were largely on your own, other people don't genuinely care about your progress, and it's hard to envision how you will ever be allowed to do anything more interesting or fulfilling than what you are doing right this moment, in the organization where you currently are. This leads to a desire to find something else, somewhere else, where you *might* have better opportunities.

In these moments, remind yourself: *this is not the dream job.* The first job or the first few jobs aren't going to be perfect. You no doubt went into college and exited upon graduation with lofty expectations, either of your own or those belonging to others, about where that college degree was going to take you. And someday, with more experience, with more education, with more clarity on who you are and what you are looking for, you will get there.

But you're not there yet. Right now it's all about gaining experience; building your skills, knowledge, and abilities; and gaining clarity on who you are, what you value about work, and where your gaps are. It's about learning how to take ownership for your career, as opposed to blaming others for not giving you what you expected. And, **it's about playing the long game**.

A while back there was a piece in *Inc.* that shared that Stephen Curry, arguably one of the best players in today's NBA, if not of all time, is the fifth highest-paid member of his team.[32] At first this seems utterly ridiculous. Surely if his current team, the Golden State Warriors, isn't willing to pony up the cash, he could take his talents to the highest bidder (and there would be plenty of those). Instead, he decided to "play the long game" with his career, recognizing there was value in staying where he was, building a brand and a reputation and a network, for an even higher long-term payout.

It turns out Curry made his current contract—worth $44 million, not exactly something to sneeze at—back in 2012, when he was injured and he wasn't the hottest thing in pro basketball. He could have gambled for something bigger and better, and, as he notes, he could have lost. Big. Instead, now he has a long-term endorsement with Under Armour, and in the summer of 2017 Curry signed a new five year, $201 million deal with the Warriors, the largest contract in NBA history.

That's exactly the mind-set you need to take with your own career. What's the long game for you? What does jumping to the next available opportunity get you, and what might you possibly lose along the way? What would staying where you are do for you in terms of short-term and long-term opportunities? You will never have a crystal ball, or all of the information you need, to make this decision. But you can and should ask yourself some key questions to start to critically assess the situation, gather some data, and analyze possible next steps.

Take a moment to reflect on these questions:

1. What do I value about my current role, organization, and location? What's missing?

2. What skills, abilities, and knowledge areas have I gained from working in this role? What do I still need to learn?

3. Are there opportunities in this organization to grow into more challenging roles I would find interesting/fulfilling?

4. What am I missing in order to grow in my career?

You may notice these questions are very similar to the first two career competencies we discussed in chapter 1: Knowing Why (individual and organizational values) and Knowing How (skills, knowledge, and abilities for current and future roles). The third career competency, Knowing Whom, is one of the tools you will use to figure out what exactly the next step should be.

Do Your Homework

It is always better to take a new job because you are moving *toward* something, as opposed to because you are escaping *from* something. When you are in the latter position, it tends to lead to a poor decision-making process: *I'll take anything if it just gets me out of here.* It encourages you to make a leap into something without doing the work to assess what the next opportunity might offer you, in terms of the long game.

Whatever your current situation, don't shortchange this critical work! No matter how bad it is, no matter how undervalued you may feel, you already *have* a job. There is no need to jump from the frying pan into the fire, as the saying goes. All that will mean is in relatively short time you will be job-hunting once again, which isn't great for your mind-set or your résumé.

This is the point at which having a robust, diverse network of mentors, wise counselors, and sponsors is critical to your path and your decision-making process. And you don't want to wait until you need those people to develop those relationships. Instead, you should work on constantly building your network, *especially* in those times when you don't need people. Informational interviews are not just for when you need a job. Start building that practice into your routine and ongoing professional and personal development activities.

The Emmy and Academy-award winning producer Brian Grazer is known not just for his work in television and movies but for his intentional practice of holding regular "curiosity conversations." Over thirty-plus years, he has reached out to individuals outside of his industry and expertise to talk about *their work* and *their lives*, to stay in a place of constant, lifelong learning.[33]

I love this practice for its utter simplicity. This is something each of us can and should do; you don't have to be a famous movie producer. Starting right now, make a habit of having these conversations once or twice a month with someone who is not in your immediate sphere of influence. Your goal is only to listen and to learn, not to ask for anything (but their time). Come with a set of prepared questions, but also be prepared to let the conversation go where it needs to go. **Stay in a place of natural curiosity.**

Here are some potential questions you might use:

- What is one "life lesson" you have learned and how did you learn it?

- If you were starting this job all over, what would you do differently and why?
- What is the biggest lesson you've learned about effective communication and how did you learn it?
- What is the biggest lesson you've learned about leadership and how did you learn it?
- What is the greatest challenge or hurdle you have had to overcome and what did you do?
- What is the greatest success you have accomplished? What did you learn?
- When faced with a complex decision or problem with no obvious solution, what steps do you take to approach it?
- How would you describe your learning style? What tools or strategies do you find particularly effective?
- What habit would you most like to change about yourself? Why?
- If you weren't afraid of failing, what would you do? Why?
- When was the last time you were surprised by something/someone? What happened?
- What were the differences between the best and worst decisions you have made?
- How do you define success? How have you (or how are you working to) achieved it?
- What is the best piece of advice you have for me?

In addition to these curiosity-conversation questions, take your answers to the Knowing Why and Knowing How questions and ask for these individuals' feedback. Your goal is not to ask them what to do, but to gather data on your decision-making processes, on your strengths and growth opportunities, and on potential next steps you could take.

Gain from the wisdom of their experience and their knowledge about future opportunities within your organization or elsewhere. Listen when they tell you what are the things you need to work on to better prepare yourself for the next step. Ultimately the decision must be yours, and yours alone. Gather as much data as you can, so when you do make that decision, it's an informed one, and not just a stab in the dark.

Another reason curiosity conversations are so valuable is that they provide critical insight into other fields, industries, and roles that may be of interest to you. It's not acceptable to just sit back and complain that you don't know of all the possibilities. Of course you don't! And no one is going to do that work for you. **Do your homework.**

If you're dissatisfied with where you live, do some research on other possible locations via the Internet and chatting with friends and acquaintances who currently live in those places. Make a list of the qualities you are looking for—big city, small town, east coast, west coast, near the mountains, near water, lots of young people, lots of people you already know, close to family, and so on—and then start looking for places that meet those criteria.

Research cost of living in those locations and how it compares to where you are now, and be thoughtful about what it will take financially for you to both make a move and to live there.

If you're looking to switch industries, use tools like Glassdoor.com to research different jobs and organizations and to see how your strengths and personality might align with different fields. Get on several job boards and scan the roles people are hiring for and take note of what piques your interest and why.

This is also a great process to start identifying the gaps you need to fill. If there is a position you are interested in that requires skills, knowledge, or abilities you don't currently possess, think about intentional steps you can start taking to fill those gaps to better position yourself for those opportunities in the future.

The bottom line is this: rarely will someone just walk up to you and hand you a job, or take you by the hand and say, "Come with me. I'm going to show you the way." And in today's world, where information is available at our fingertips, it is unacceptable to say you did not do your homework. Ask for help; you don't have to do it on your own. Reach out to your mentors and your sponsors for advice and guidance. You might want to seek out the guidance of a professional career coach.

But own your future and your decisions.

Assess Your Options

Making the decision it's time to make a change and actually making a change are two very different things. Here you may find you run into one of several situations:

1. You're ready for the change, you can identify generally what it is, and you're paralyzed with the (perceived) options available to you.
2. You're ready for the change, you can identify what it is, and you're not qualified to get there.
3. You're ready for the change, but you can't quite identify what it is or how to get there.
4. The change has been presented to you and you're not sure if you're ready or qualified.

Let's take these one by one.

You're ready for the change, you can identify generally what it is, and you're paralyzed with the (perceived) options available to you.

You're ready to make a change, and you can see some future potential place where you would like to end up (you think), but you're unclear which path to take to get there. Indeed, you may be suffering from what's called "analysis-paralysis," spending so much time analyzing all of the potential next steps you could make (and their potential outcomes) that you never just pick one. Or you have set your sights on too high or too vague of a goal and find there are hundreds of different paths that could potentially lead to your goal.

This is along the lines of what our friend, Alexa, was going through in chapter 1. She thought she wanted to be in sales and marketing, she knew she wanted to do something more creative, but she wasn't sure what her next step should be. When framed that way, it can be overwhelming. How many different roles can you find that incorporate sales and marketing? How many different industries? In how many different locations? How do you get from some vague notion of what you might do to a very specific next step you can act upon?

Sometimes there is value in *removing* possibilities. Are there locations where you really won't go? Then take them off the list. Is it important you work in a specific type of industry or organization? Then remove the ones that don't fit into that category. Is there a particular skill area you're looking to develop? Then remove the available positions that don't provide that opportunity.

Finally, remember the world is not, in fact, your oyster. It may seem like you have a thousand possible doors open to you, but that's not at all true. There are jobs and industries you wouldn't like or be good at doing. These are your nonoptions. You either don't have the experience, the qualifications, or the interest to make most things a good fit. And don't overthink this next step. Go back to your reflective practices. What do you want more of, or less of, compared to your current role? What would be challenging and continue to grow and develop your skills? What do your mentors and sponsors recommend you consider? Whatever that is, chances are it's a good next step.

This doesn't mean a job offer is going to fall into your lap. You still have to do the work of setting up curiosity conversations, identifying job leads, and submitting applications. But by narrowing the universe of possible options, engaging your network in your decision making, and creating an intentional plan, you are in a much stronger position.

You're ready for the change, you can identify what it is, and you're not qualified to get there.

So what if you can identify that ideal next step, but you realize you're not qualified for it? This happens quite often, in fact. Rarely will the opportunity land in your lap that is perfectly written for your skill set and your experience. The first step is to check your assumptions. Are you truly not qualified, or are you suffering from a bit of the impostor syndrome, and talking yourself out of it? This is where great mentors can help you and give objective feedback on how your skill set may or may not align with the role.

But if you truly do not meet the qualifications, then you must ask yourself what steps you can take to correct those deficiencies and fill those gaps. It may mean asking for stretch assignments in your current role to gain needed experience. It may mean pursuing additional credentials or even a graduate degree. It may mean finding a volunteer opportunity outside of work that broadens your résumé and your network. It will most certainly require an investment of time and possibly resources by you. But this is an investment in your future, and a valuable one.

One practice I would recommend that you start incorporating into your habits is to constantly survey the landscape for potential opportunities. Just like you should make a practice of regularly conducting curiosity conversations, *before* you need to ask someone for help with a job search, you should constantly be looking at other opportunities *before* you are ready to pursue something different. Sign up for several search engines that will automatically send you openings in the field, industry, or location of your interest.

Doing so gives you a sense of what people are looking for and the areas you need to grow and develop, which is additional data you can start to act upon. It also gives you insider knowledge into what your competitors are doing, which will only be helpful to you in your current role. The most frustrating time to look for a job is when you are desperate for a job. Always be looking, and then the opportunities will come to you, and likely when you least expect them.

You're ready for the change, but you can't quite identify what it is or how to get there.

This leads to the third scenario, when you're ready for a change but you're not sure what, or how to get there. This is, clearly, the weakest position to be in, and largely reflective of the fact that you have not been doing your homework. But there's no time like the present to start! Go back to the questions presented earlier in this chapter, and do some deep reflection about what you do and don't like, what your skills are, and what challenges you are looking for. Scan the landscape and take note of which positions grab your attention and why. Reach out to mentors for advice and counsel, and set up curiosity conversations to increase your knowledge about what type of opportunities exist and to start building your network.

It's not going to happen overnight, but if you don't start doing the work, then six months from now, you will find yourself in the exact same place you are in now. So start from that place: where do you want to be in six months or a year? Once you have an answer to that question, start working backwards to put a plan into place to get there.

The change has been presented to you, and you're not sure if you're ready or qualified.

Finally, you may run into a situation where someone brings you an opportunity you were neither expecting nor looking for, and you're not sure if you're either qualified or ready for it. Or you may question if the timing is right, and if you should walk away from the position you're currently in, and miss out on possible opportunities there, for an unknown but seemingly great opportunity somewhere else. In some ways this is the best scenario, because you have had to do very little work and someone is tapping you on the shoulder and offering to bring you along with them. But it also requires some hard assessment and possibly some difficult conversations with people who are currently investing in you.

Once more, you need to gather additional data, both on your current role and on this new opportunity. What new skills and abilities will you gain from the new role? What will you learn and how will it challenge you? What new doors will it open for you? Similarly, with your current role, what are the promotional opportunities in your future? Are you still being challenged, still learning, or can you do that job with your eyes closed at this point? Are there opportunities in the future there you can't yet see?

There is never anything wrong with taking a new opportunity to your current employer, to ask about how it compares to where you are currently. But please note: *this does not mean your current employer will react well to this news.* If you are fortunate, you work for an organization that is focused on growing and developing its people, and understands that sometimes that means people have to spread their wings and go elsewhere. But sometimes people's egos are too large to take this approach. Some may feel this is a betrayal of their trust and their investment in you and that you are not grateful for the opportunities you have been given.

There is absolutely nothing you can do about how other people react to you. You can only control your own behavior, your own attitude, and your own reactions to others. The irony here, of course, is the place that is focused on your growth and development, whether you stay with them or not, is actually the place where you probably should think about staying.

(See how that works?) But you should not let a potential negative reaction from your supervisor or others keep you from gathering the data you need to make an informed decision. Just don't go into that conversation blindly. Be prepared for how others may react. And if it truly concerns you, then seek out other mentors and sponsors for feedback.

As you are assessing the pros and cons of these choices, do not be charmed by potential financial gains, or turn your nose up at an opportunity that does not seem to reward you monetarily. There are many other rewards that can be far more valuable than money, including growth of your résumé, connections, opportunity to do "meaningful" work, opportunity to live in a place you love, opportunity to live your values, and so on. Money is not unimportant; you want to be able to pay your bills, save for your future, and have some fun. But don't make this the overriding consideration, so that you turn down a chance to build your future for the benefit of a nicer apartment, fancier stuff, or better vacations now.

Remember: the only time a raise is motivating is the first time it hits your paycheck. After that, your life simply expands to fill that space, and you no longer see or feel its effects.

There's an old saying: **don't let perfect be the enemy of the good.** Basically, what this means is, don't get so fixated on trying to be perfect when good enough will do. Don't be so fixated on finding the "perfect" job, which does not exist, by the way, that you pass up really great opportunities to learn and to grow and to get started in your career. Don't be so blinded by a flashy office or title or marketing campaign that you forget to notice what it is you will be doing, day in and day out. Sometimes the smaller, seemingly less prestigious opportunity is the better one, because it offers more opportunities to actually do the work.

Keep your focus on the intrinsic rewards. Play the long game.

Tell Your Story

Part of owning what's next is being able to tell your story. How are the experiences you are having and the choices you are making creating a compelling narrative about who you are, what you can do, and where you are headed? How does your résumé—both in print and online via LinkedIn or another portfolio—tell your story? If someone were to pick that up and look at it without context from you, what will they learn about you?

It can be hard at times to project forward. Many of the jobs you will hold in the future have not been created yet. It is the era of the generalist: someone who has a broad understanding of and ability to implement multiple skill sets. These include written and oral communications, a global mind-set, conflict management, decision making and problem-solving, an ability to critically analyze and synthesize information and data, innovation and creativity, working in teams, an entrepreneurial mind-set, and many others that today's employers indicate they are looking for in their employees, and they find many young professionals in particular are lacking.[34]

Your job with your professional résumé is to demonstrate, through your experiences, and education, how you are progressively building these skills and how you have been able to apply them to achieve results. You need to tell your story, effectively and strategically.

The nice thing about a professional résumé versus a college résumé is that you are no longer limited to the one-page rule. But that does not give you license to be sloppy with it. And just like in college, you may need to tailor your résumé to meet the specific criteria of different positions.

For example, if you are applying for a role in education, then you should put your educational credentials at the top, before diving into your experiences. For roles outside of education, it is acceptable to put your educational credentials at the end, and to focus on experience first. Depending on what the role is looking for, you might choose to focus on different aspects of different projects; for example, your ability to grow and lead teams, your ability to manage projects, your ability to generate revenue and manage budgets. **What is the story you need to tell about yourself to this employer?** Critically examine the job description's duties or essential functions and qualifications sections for insight into how to answer this question.

Strategically telling your story also means it's time to let go of some activities from your résumé. Sorry, but no one's going to be *that* interested that you were social chair of your sorority anymore or that you studied abroad for a semester in Italy, unless it helps to tell your story for this position.

In most cases, people will be far more interested in your most recent professional experiences since you graduated. And these include volunteer experiences. If you spent four years in college tutoring at-risk youth, but in the five years since graduation, you have not demonstrated meaningful commitment to any organization that is outside of yourself and your work, then you cannot tell a story that includes a commitment to giving back and supporting underprivileged children. If that is a gap you need to fill, then you need to think about how you can acquire tangible experiences now to do that.

Generally speaking, the sections you should include on a professional résumé are the following:

- **Full Name and Contact Information**—a current phone number and e-mail address will suffice, and unless you are OK with someone contacting you at your current place of employment, it should be a personal phone and e-mail address.

- **Education**—degree, school, and year you graduated. If you graduated with honors you can include that as well. You can also put any certifications or credentials you have received here or put those in a separate section later.

- **Work Experience**—in reverse chronological (most recent experience first) order, include all of your professional work experience from present day to graduation. If you had meaningful employment while you were in college you can include that as well, but no one expects you to do so. Include your position title, place of employment, and the dates you worked there. Under each of these headings, use bullet points to describe your role and your activities with short, action-oriented statements that demonstrate impact, and describe how you applied skills and knowledge. *Only your current role should be in present tense*; all other roles should be in past tense. An example of a work-experience descriptor should read as follows:

o "Managed cross-functional team of five staff members to create and implement an organizational-satisfaction survey. Collected and analyzed results and presented recommended-action items to senior leadership." This descriptor is short and to the point, action-oriented, and demonstrates an ability to lead teams, work with data, analyze and synthesize information, and communicate with senior leaders. That's a great story to tell!

- **Service/Volunteer Experience**—again, put these in reverse chronological order. Include your role, the organization, and the dates of service. If warranted, you can add additional descriptors that continue telling your story, but keep these short.

- **Presentations and Publications**—if you have presented at conferences or had papers or articles published, be sure to include these with full and appropriate attribution.

- **Awards and Honors**—if you have received any professional or civic honors or awards, include these with the name of the award, the organization who awarded it, and the date it was received.

- **Technical Skills**—highlight any technical skills you possess, in particular unique skills like mastery of data-analytics software, web-design software, content-management software, and others. Pay attention to the skills the job is looking for, and note the ones you possess. You can mention Microsoft Suite here, but that is a general baseline expectation and will not make you stand out from the crowd.

It should be noted that if you are applying for academic (faculty) jobs, then a very different sort of CV, which is focused primarily on teaching and research experience, is required and should be created for those positions. Additionally, certain fields like the arts require very specific résumés or portfolios that do not align with the basic professional outline presented above. In all cases, seek out guidance from mentors or others working in the field to make sure you are presenting yourself in the manner that is most appropriate to that field.

At some point you may find yourself with time gaps in your résumé, whether through your own making or otherwise. In these moments, continue filling your time with "productive" experiences, whether through volunteering or consulting or education, if your goal is to return to the workforce. This is not the place to discuss the fairness of this need; you should just be aware that hiring managers will look upon résumé gaps in a negative light and as a lack of experience, which puts you in a more challenging position to tell your story.

As you grow your career, your professional résumé will continue growing, and over time some things toward the beginning of your career may start dropping off, or you may start shortening the descriptor statements. People are always going to be more interested in what you have been doing most recently. And that is why you can never stop building your skills and abilities and seeking out experiences that challenge you.

One strategy I would advise is to build in regular time—quarterly or every six months—to update your résumé. This doesn't mean you need to make it perfect, but make sure you are adding in your current projects, roles, and responsibilities so you don't lose them down the road. You'll be amazed at how quickly you will forget things that are valuable parts of your career journey.

You want your résumé to tell a story. Not a made-up fabrication of a life that does not exist, but the true story of who you are and what you can do. And remember, once you're hired you will have to demonstrate in action that what you said about yourself is true. Your professional résumé, in print and online, is a reflection of who you are, not a projection of who you want to be.

Navigate Life and Relationship Changes

As you move into your middle and late twenties, your experiences will start shaping your life decisions as well as those related to your career. You will become clearer on the type of life you want to create, where you want to create it, and with whom. Decisions about marriage and children, as we discussed previously in chapter 3, will become more urgent and important.

You may find that your ability to jump at a professional opportunity is no longer just about you but is affected by its potential impact on a significant other or children. When you take responsibility for creating a family, the consequences of your decisions are no longer just about you.

When you start factoring another person into your decisions, you begin to realize that your decisions will require some compromise and trade-offs. For example, if you are offered a great professional opportunity across the country, will your significant other be able to find something of equivalent reward or stature, or is he or she willing to take a step back in his or her career goals, to support yours? If, together, you decide to pursue career or life opportunities in a location with a significantly higher cost of living, what will that mean about how it impacts your lifestyle and the financial choices you will need to make? If you decide to have children, how will that impact your financial and professional choices?

This latter dilemma is one that many young people don't think of factoring into their planning. There are real financial consequences to having children, of course, which include everything from diapers to day care to sports camps to college. You likely will never have the financial security to feel comfortable covering all of these costs *before* having children, but with some careful planning you can make sure you approach this decision with responsibility and care.

But there are also some unspoken identity consequences many young adults don't think about prior to becoming "mom" or "dad." Because women in this country still do the bulk of the caretaking, these identity issues tend to impact women to a greater degree than they do men. Women who choose to (or have to) continue to work full-time after children continue to do the bulk of the housework and child care. Women and men who choose to (or are able to) work part-time or become stay-at-home moms or dads are faced with potentially losing their professional identities in addition to their paychecks.[35] The emotional toll of this choice can often be steep and unexpected.

As you navigate through these decisions and transitions, take the time to seek out wise counselors, mentors, and role models. Find people who have walked in these shoes before you, and talk to them about how they managed it. Seek out groups of people who are in a similar stage of life to share challenges and successes. And, if you have a partner, engage him or her in the process. Share how you are feeling and talk about how you can reset expectations, boundaries, and the division of work, both at home and at the office.

As you move into this next stage, you will find that the administrative details of your life will start becoming more complex. Home ownership, investments, and dependents are just a few of the things that will require you to seek out more nuanced and expert tax advice. Life insurance and powers of attorney become necessities. In all of these areas, just know that there are experts out there who can help and advise you. Don't be afraid to ask questions and to seek the counsel you need.

In addition to seeking out mentors for yourself, another transition you can expect to experience is that to the role of mentor and wise counselor for others. As you gain experience and grow your career, you will start taking on leadership and management roles, and be responsible for the career paths of other, mostly younger employees. **Do not take this role lightly!** Reflect on those supervisors and mentors whom you have looked up to and admired for the ways they developed and invested in you. Think about how you might emulate those traits moving forward. Remember the ones who did not support you as well as you would have liked, and think about how that made you feel.

It can be tempting, after all of the work you have done to get to where you are, to think others should have to figure it out for themselves too, in a sort of weird professional hazing process. Let me be clear: *there is no value in this.* We do no one any good, not ourselves, not our organizations, not our peers and subordinates, when we refuse to show others the way. There are lessons to be learned from experience, certainly, and you never want to rob someone else of the opportunity to learn those lessons because you are always swooping in to save them. But true leaders and mentors always shine a light on the path and look for ways they can walk beside people along it.

We all need mentors, and your need for growth and development won't end here. Throughout your career and life journey, you should look for and seek ways to attract mentors and wise counselors into your life. But we all can also be mentors, and you should look for opportunities to support the paths of others. It's not enough to only reach up and across. Part of your responsibility is to reach down as well, and to bring others with you. That's being an adult. That's owning what's next.

Create Your Plan

As a final step, now that you have spent all of this time reflecting on your values, your strengths and growth opportunities, the life and the community you are creating, it's time to create a plan for the next few years, *a living document* you can take with you. It's a living document because it should be revisited at regular intervals and amended as needed according to changes in your life and your career. And it is a living document in that **you should live it**, intentionally and thoughtfully. Seek out feedback and guidance from your mentors, sponsors, and wise counselors on the steps you are taking to move forward in your life.

It's your life and you have to own it. But none of us are on this journey alone.

Five-Year Vision

Start by creating a five-year vision for yourself. This is not a goal statement, but a descriptive statement, an image of where you want to be, an aspiration to keep in mind for your future. You can write it in full sentences, in bullets, in images, or whatever works for you.

Where do you see yourself in five years…

Professionally?

Personally?

One-Year Goals to Move You Toward the Vision

Now that you have an image for where you would like to end up, it's time to get more specific and think about some strategic steps you can take in the next year to get closer to your vision. Remember: no more than one year.

Write two to three SMART goals related to developing your skills, knowledge, and abilities. What do you need to acquire or do in order to get closer to your professional vision?

Write one to two SMART goals related to your well-being and financial management. What will you do to own these two areas of your life over the next year?

Write one to two SMART goals related to building community and relationships. What do you need to do in the next year to get closer to your personal vision?

Who will you reach out to, to gather feedback on your progress toward your goals? Who will keep you accountable? When will you reach out to them to share this plan with them?

When will you revisit this plan?

Final Thoughts

This book has been about navigating the sometimes challenging, frustrating, uncertain transition from college to life after college. Over the past five chapters, we have looked at how you can and should work, build a life, create community, practice reflection, and own what's next. You've been pushed to reflect on your values, strengths, and opportunities for growth; identify your gaps; and create intentional strategies to fill those gaps. None of these are prescriptions for a perfect or successful life. Indeed, I would argue, there is no such thing. Life is messy and complicated and imperfect. Success can only be defined by you.

I hope as you go on from here that you will consider yourself a lifelong learner in every sense of that term. Use *every experience*, every setback, and every unexpected door that opens as an opportunity to learn: about yourself, about others, about your community, and about the world. Be open to new perspectives and points of view. Surround yourself with people who don't think the way you do, and ask them to share their experiences with you. Listen and learn from them. Before you say no to things, try saying yes and why not. Dare to take a leap and believe that the net you need will, in fact, appear.

As you move forward, remember these five key phrases: "Do the Work"; "Build a Life"; "Create Community"; "Practice Reflection"; "Own What's Next." Use them as your guideposts and wise counsel when you need them. But remember, you have everything you need inside of you, right now, to create a successful life.

Most importantly, no matter how thoughtful and intentional you decide to be, make room for fun and whimsy. Do things that push you out of your comfort zone. Keep company with people who make you laugh. Travel to places you've never been before. Don't delay joy. Practice gratitude.

You get this one life, and only you get to live it. Challenging, frustrating, and uncertain, yes. But also exciting, surprising, and filled with wonder. It is exactly what you make of it. It starts today.

Practice Reflection

1. What did you think or feel when you read Andrew's story?

2. What do you need to do to "play the long game" with your career and life?

3. How does the idea of "The Four-Year Career" strike you? How do you feel about change?

4. What's been the most challenging about your adult relationships?

5. How will you use this knowledge about yourself in the next year?

KEY TAKEAWAYS, IDEAS,
AND ACTION ITEMS

NOTES

1. For a discussion on issues related to the transition from college to life after college, see: C. P. Niemiec, R. M. Ryan, and E. L. Deci, "The Path Taken: Consequences of Attaining Intrinsic and Extrinsic Aspirations in Postcollege Life," *Journal of Research in Personality* 43 (2009): 291–306, doi:10.1016/j.jrp.2008.09.001; V. Cohen-Scali, "The Influence of Family, Social, and Work Socialization on the Construction of Professional Identity of Young Adults," *Journal of Career Development* 29, no. 4 (2003): 237–49, doi:10.1177/089484530302900402; J. J. Arnett, "Emerging Adulthood: What Is It, and What Is It Good For?," *Child Development Perspectives* 1, no. 2 (2007): 68–73, doi:10.1111/j.1750-8606.2007.00016.x; J. E. Schulenberg, A. J. Sameroff, and D. Cicchetti, "The Transition to Adulthood as a Critical Juncture in the Course of Psychopathology and Mental Health," *Development and Psychopathology* 16 (2004): 799–806, doi:10.10170S0954579404040015.

2. J. C. Maxwell, *Mentoring 101* (Nashville, TN: Thomas Nelson, 2008), 61.

3. J. J. Arnett, "Emerging Adulthood: A Theory of Development from the Late Teens through the Twenties," *American Psychologist* 55, no. 5 (2000): 469–80.

4. For just two examples of this disconnect, see: Hart Research Associates, *Falling Short? College Learning and Career Success* (Washington, DC: Association of American Colleges & Universities, 2015), https://www.aacu.org/leap/public-opinion-research/2015-survey-falling-short (accessed July 1, 2017); CBI, *Inspiring Growth: CBI/Pearson Education and Skills Survey 2015* (London: CBI, 2015), http://www.cbi.org.uk/insight-and-analysis/inspiring-growth-the-education-and-skills-survey-2015/ (accessed July 1, 2017).

5. R. Fry, "Millennials Aren't Job Hopping Any Faster than Generation X Did," Pew Research Center, April 19, 2017, http://www.pewresearch.org/fact-tank/2017/04/19/millennials-arent-job-hopping-any-faster-than-generation-x-did/ (accessed July 1, 2017).

6. Deloitte, "The 2016 Deloitte Millennial Survey: Winning over the Next Generation of Leaders," 2016, https://www2.deloitte.com/content/dam/Deloitte/global/Docume nts/About-Deloitte/gx-millenial-survey-2016-exec-summary.pdf (accessed July 1, 2017).

7. A. McCaig, "Study Identified Factors that Lead to Greater College Success," *Rice University News Release*, May 30, 2017, http://news.rice.edu/2017/05/30/study-identifies-factors-that-lead-to-greater-college-success/ (accessed July 1, 2017).

8. For more information on the "boundaryless career," see: R. J. Defillippi and M. B. Arthur, "The Boundaryless Career: A Competency-based Perspective," *Journal of Organizational Behavior* 15, no. 4 (1994): 307–24, doi: https://doi.org/10.1002/job.4030150403; see also, S. C. de Janasz, S. E. Sullivan, V. Whiting, and E. Biech, "Mentor Networks and Career Success: Lessons for Turbulent Times" (Executive Commentary), *The Academy of Management Executive (1993–2005)* 17, no. 4 (2003): 78–93, doi:10.5465/ame.2003.11851850.

9. S. Sandberg, *Lean In: Women, Work and the Will to Lead* (New York: Alfred A. Knopf, 2013); A. Slaughter, "Why Women Still Can't Have It All," *The Atlantic*, July/August 2012, http://www.theatlantic.com/magazine/archive/2012/07/why-women-still-cant-have-it-all/309020/ (accessed July 1, 2017).

10. EY, "Global Generations: A Global Study on Work-Life Challenges Across Generations," 2015, http://www.ey.com/Publication/vwLUAssets/EY-global-generations-a-global-study-on-work-life-challenges-across-generations/$FILE/EY-global-generations-a-global-study-on-work-life-challenges-across-generations.pdf (accessed July 1, 2017).

11. K. Loria, "23 Incredible Benefits of Getting More Sleep," *Business Insider*, December 22, 2014, http://www.businessinsider.com/why-sleep-is-important-2014-12 (accessed July 1, 2017).

12. J. Coleman and J. Coleman, "The Upside of Downtime," *Harvard Business Review*, December 6, 2012, https://hbr.org/2012/12/the-upside-of-downtime (accessed July 1, 2017).

13. B. Berkowitz and P. Clark, "The Health Hazards of Sitting," *The Washington Post*, January 20, 2014, https://www.washingtonpost.com/apps/g/page/national/the-health-hazards-of-sitting/750/ (accessed July 1, 2017).

14. See, for example: J. Cornfield, "Millennials Slow to Start Investing in Stock Market, Bankrate Survey Finds," *Bankrate*, July 6, 2016, http://www.bankrate.com/investing/millennials-slow-to-start-investing-in-stock-market-bankrate-survey-finds/ (accessed July 1, 2017); Wells Fargo, "2016 Wells Fargo Retirement Study," 2016, https://www08.wellsfargomedia.com/assets/pdf/commercial/retirement-employee-benefits/perspectives/2016-millennial-retirement-study.pdf (accessed July 1, 2017); B. Steverman, "Millennials Are Freaking over Retirement—And Not Doing Much About It," *Bloomberg*, August 16, 2016, https://www.bloomberg.com/news/articles/2016-08-16/millennials-are-freaking-over-retirement-and-not-doing-much-about-it (accessed July 1, 2017).

15. S. Achor, *The Happiness Advantage* (New York: Virgin Books, 2011), 78.

16. B. Brown, *Daring Greatly* (New York: Avery, 2012), 71.

17. G. Cook, "Why We Are Wired to Connect," *Scientific American*, October 22, 2013, https://www.scientificamerican.com/article/why-we-are-wired-to-connect/ (accessed July 1, 2017).

18. Achor, *The Happiness Advantage*, 176.

19. M. S. Granovetter, "The Strength of Weak Ties," *American Journal of Sociology* 78, no. 6 (1973): 1360–80, doi:10.1086/225469.

20. A. M. Grant, *Give and Take: Why Helping Others Drives Our Success* (New York: Penguin, 2014).

21. For resources on age and fertility, see: Mayo Clinic Staff, "Pregnancy after 35: Healthy Moms, Healthy Babies," Mayo Clinic, July 29, 2014, http://www.mayoclinic.org/healthy-lifestyle/getting-pregnant/in-depth/pregnancy/art-20045756 (accessed July 1, 2017); Southern California Center for Reproductive Medicine, "How Age Affects Fertility," 2017, http://www.socalfertility.com/fertility-resources/age-and-fertility-infographic/ (accessed July 1, 2017).

22. S. Godin, *Tribes: We Need You to Lead Us* (New York: Portfolio, 2008), 1–2, 26–27.

23. For a discussion on the science behind neuroplasticity, see: T. Adams, "Norman Doidge: The Man Teaching Us to Change Our Minds," *The Guardian*, February 8, 2015, https://www.theguardian.com/science/2015/feb/08/norman-doidge-brain-healing-neuroplasticity-interview (accessed July 1, 2017); J. L. Kays, R. A. Hurley, and K. H. Taber, "The Dynamic Brain:

Neuroplasticity and Mental Health," *The Journal of Neuropsychiatry and Clinical Neurosciences* 24, no. 2 (2012): 118–24, doi:10.1176/appi.neuropsych.12050109.

24. For a discussion on the myth of effective multitasking, see: S. Mautz, "Psychology and Neuroscience Blow Up the Myth of Effective Multitasking," *Inc.*, May 11, 2017, https://www.inc.com/scott-mautz/psychology-and-neuroscience-blow-up-the-myth-of-effective-multitasking.html?cid=sf01001&sr_share=twitter (accessed July 1, 2017); J. Wihbey, "Multitasking, Social Media and Distraction: Research Review," *Journalist's Resource*, July 11, 2013, https://journalistsresource.org/studies/society/social-media/multitasking-social-media-distraction-what-does-research-say (accessed July 1, 2017).

25. M. Buckingham and C. Coffman, *First, Break All the Rules: What the World's Great Managers Do Differently* (New York: Simon & Schuster, 1999).

26. C. Dweck, "What Is Mindset?," Mindset, http://mindsetonline.com/whatisit/about/index.html (accessed July 1, 2017).

27. T. Bradberry and J. Greaves, *Emotional Intelligence 2.0* (San Diego, CA: TalentSmart, 2009), 21–22.

28. Ibid., 17.

29. J. M. Kouzes and B. Z. Posner, *Learning Leadership* (San Francisco, CA: Wiley, 2016), 100.

30. See, for example: J. Meister, "The Future of Work: Job Hopping Is the 'New Normal' for Millennials," *Forbes*, August 14, 2012, https://www.forbes.com/sites/jeannemeister/2012/08/14/the-

future-of-work-job-hopping-is-the-new-normal-for-
millennials/#601aba3513b8 (accessed July 1, 2017); Fry, "Millennials
Aren't Job Hopping any Faster than Generation X Did."

31. A. Kamenetz, "The Four-Year Career," Fast Company, January 12,
    2012, https://www.fastcompany.com/1802731/four-year-career
    (accessed July 1, 2017).

32. Z. Henry, "Why Stephen Curry Plays the Long Game with His
    Finances," *Inc.*, March 23, 2016, https://www.inc.com/zoe-
    henry/stephen-curry-plays-the-long-game-finance-strategy.html
    (accessed July 1, 2017); T, Reynolds, "Stephen Curry Gets 'Biggest
    Contract in NBA History'," *Bloomberg*, July 1, 2017,
    https://www.bloomberg.com/news/articles/2017-07-02/day-1-
    curry-gets-huge-deal-hayward-hears-heat-sales-pitch (accessed July 3,
    2017).

33. B. Grazer, *A Curious Mind: The Secret to a Bigger Life* (New York: Simon
    & Schuster, 2016).

34. Hart Research Associates, *Falling Short?*

35. For a great discussion of the care-giving versus career debate, see: A.
    Slaughter, *Unfinished Business* (New York: Penguin Random House,
    2015).

ACKNOWLEDGEMENTS

Much gratitude is owed to the following:

Those who read early editions of this book and provided valuable feedback, insight, and encouragement: Stephanie Bandyk, Lauren Beam, Megan Bosworth, Kate Brooks, Andy Chan, Maureen Early, Elizabeth Garrett, Ryan Howard, Matt Imboden, Jessica Long, Matthew Phillips, Ryan Smith, Kimberly Struglinski, Patrick Sullivan, and Tiffany Waddell Tate. Your time is appreciated, your advice made this book better, and your never-ending support motivates me every day.

Bill Kane, for shepherding this project to and through publication, and for having such a great sense of humor and perspective on what really matters.

Tommy Brown and Carter Cook for your wisdom, insight, feedback, and perspective.

The Wake Forest University Office of Personal and Career Development for giving me the opportunity and freedom to pursue a project such as this.

My family, for giving me the tools, resources, and the push that I need, when I need it.

All of the young professionals and college students whose stories helped to shape the ideas that are in these pages. Specific names and details have been changed. Your wisdom, courage, and willingness to share with me and with one another, as you do this thing called life, is nothing less than inspirational. This book would not have happened without you, and my work and life are richer for having shared a small part of your journeys with you. This book is for you.

ABOUT THE AUTHOR

Allison E. McWilliams is Assistant Vice President, Mentoring and Alumni Personal & Career Development within the Office of Personal & Career Development at Wake Forest University. In these roles, she leads and provides training, support, guidance, and resources for formal and informal mentoring relationships for college students, faculty and staff, and alumni, as well as leading personal and career development programs for young professionals. She has written for and spoken to national and international audiences about effective mentoring strategies, leadership, and professional development.

Prior to joining Wake Forest in 2010, Allison was a public service faculty member at the University of Georgia, where she created, administered, and served as a facilitator for leadership development and organizational development programs for higher education and public sector audiences. Allison earned her bachelor's degree from Wake Forest, and holds a master's in public relations and a doctorate in higher education administration from the University of Georgia.